Six Novelists

CARNEGIE SERIES IN ENGLISH—NUMBER FIVE

STENDHAL
DOSTOEVSKI
TOLSTOY
HARDY
DREISER
PROUST

Six Novelists

by William M. Schutte
John A. Hart
Edward A. Trainor
Robert C. Slack
Donald M. Goodfellow
James T. Steen

Essay Index Reprint Series

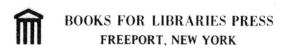
BOOKS FOR LIBRARIES PRESS
FREEPORT, NEW YORK

Library of Congress Cataloging in Publication Data

Carnegie Institute of Technology, Pittsburgh. Dept. of
   English.
   Six novelists: Stendhal, Dostoevski, Tolstoy, Hardy,
Dreiser, Proust.

   (Essay index reprint series)
   Original ed. issued as no. 5 of the Carnegie series
in English.
   1. Fiction--19th century--Addresses, essays,
lectures. 2. Fiction--20th century--Addresses, essays,
lectures. I. Schutte, William M. II. Series:
Carnegie series in English, no. 5.
[PN3499.C3 1972]   809.3'3   72-1311
ISBN 0-8369-2837-7

Acknowledgments

STENDHAL Quoted passages are reprinted from *Stendhal: Scarlet and Black*, translated by M. R. B. Shaw, published by Penguin Books Inc., 3300 Clipper Mill Road, Baltimore, Maryland.

DOSTOEVSKI Quoted passages are reprinted from the Constance Garnett translations of *The Brothers Karamazov* and *Crime and Punishment*, and from David Magarshack's Introduction to and translation of *The Best Short Stories of Dostoevsky*: all in The Modern Library, published by Random House, New York.

TOLSTOY The following have been used: the Constance Garnett translation of *War and Peace* in The Modern Library, published by Random House, New York; the Rosemary Edmonds translation of *Anna Karenin*, published by Penguin Books, Baltimore; Volume I of *The Complete Works of Count Tolstoy*, published by Dana Estes and Co., Boston, 1904.

HARDY The poem "The Oxen" is reprinted with the kind permission of The Macmillan Company, New York, from *Collected Poems of Thomas Hardy*, copyright, 1943; a number of quoted passages are reprinted from Florence E. Hardy's *The Later Years of Thomas Hardy*, 1930, also published by The Macmillan Company, New York.

DREISER Quoted passages are reprinted from: *A Book About Myself*, second edition, 1922, published by Boni and Liveright, Inc., New York; *Sister Carrie*, 1946, published by The World Publishing Co., Cleveland; *An American Tragedy*, 1929, published by Horace Liveright, New York; *The Bulwark*, Book Find Club Edition, 1946, published by Doubleday and Co., Inc., New York.

PROUST Quoted passages are reprinted from *Swann's Way*, copyright, 1956, by The Modern Library; *Within a Budding Grove*, copyright, 1951, by Random House, Inc.; *The Guermantes Way*, copyright, 1952, by Random House, Inc.; *The Past Recaptured*, copyright, 1932, by Albert and Charles Boni, Inc.: all in The Modern Library published by Random House, Inc., New York, and used with the kind permission of Random House.

Foreword

Annually for some years the Department of English at Carnegie Institute of Technology has presented on the campus a series of lectures on literary subjects. The present volume in the Carnegie Series in English consists of a selection of those lectures.

The audiences which gather to hear the annual English Department series comprise students and faculty from all colleges of Carnegie, along with some interested members of the Pittsburgh community. Thus the lectures here presented were offered from the platform and are now offered in print not as specialized scholarly studies but as critical commentaries designed to illuminate authors and their works for the general reader. By and large they retain in print the form in which they were delivered. They were prepared for the press by an editorial committee consisting of Norman Knox (Chairman), A. Fred Sochatoff, and Neal Woodruff, Jr. Detailed reference to all sources has not been provided, but the sources of extensive quotation are made clear under Acknowledgments.

Publication of this volume has been made possible by a grant from the Wherrett Memorial Fund of the Pittsburgh Foundation. For this vital assistance the Department of English is deeply grateful.

Austin Wright, *Head*

Department of English

Contents

Six Novelists

JULIEN SOREL

THE ENERGETIC IDEALIST IN A DESPOTIC SOCIETY

WILLIAM M. SCHUTTE

WHEN THE BODY OF HENRI BEYLE, who died in Paris on March 23, 1842, was brought to the grave, it was accompanied by three solitary mourners. At the time, one would hardly have held as an investment a first edition of either of his two long novels, which he had signed "Stendhal," one of the 171 pseudonyms which Dryasdust tells us he used. His books had had moderate, but irregular sales. Even with the provocative title *De L'Amour,* one of those most interesting to modern readers had sold a grand total of seventeen copies. His death was virtually unnoticed: two Paris papers printed brief notices (one of which misspelled his real name and, ironically enough, gave as his pen name the title of a recent best seller—" Frederic Styndall"). One of the few essays which mentioned him in the year after his death granted him at most "only one or two readers in each generation."

But Henri Beyle knew better. "Literary fame," he used to say, "is a lottery . . . I am taking a ticket whose winning number is 1935." His choice of date was startlingly accurate. Literary *interest,* to be sure, burgeoned in France during the 1880's when scholars discovered his literary remains—including some of his finest work—in the library at Grenoble, his birthplace. But literary fame—widespread acceptance—came later, and reached a peak when liberty in France was crushed, as it had been in his day, by the weight of oppression.

For Stendhal's novels are, among other things, studies of the world that totalitarianism creates. In both *The Red and the Black* and *The Charterhouse of Parma,* he presents an immensely detailed evocation of a world controlled by despotism. Indeed, as Eric Auerbach has pointed out, "Insofar as the serious realism of modern times cannot represent man otherwise than as embedded in a total reality—political, social, and economic— . . . Stendhal is its founder." And into the total reality of the despotic world which he recreates in each book, Stendhal injects protagonists whose vigor, energy, and imagination inevitably threaten to undermine the foundations on which that world is based. The totalitarian world, as he sees it, is a world of unutterable dulness, pettiness, mediocrity. Into it come men and women who are exciting, idealistic, and brilliant. The interaction of this society and these individuals is the matter of Stendhal's two great comic novels, the earlier and less complex of which I shall discuss here. But before we come to *The Red and the Black*, we must know something about the man who created it and the world in which he lived.

Born just six years before the French Revolution, at Grenoble in the mountainous country near the Italian border, Henri Beyle had a very unhappy childhood. His mother, whom he adored, died when he was seven; he was raised unloved by his wealthy bourgeois father, his pious, prudish aunt, and a fanatic Jesuit priest. Since these three were passionate royalists, Henri understandably became an even more passionate republican. At the time of the Terror, he ostentatiously paraded the tricolor through his father's house, sneaked off to republican meetings, and wrote on the wall of his room, "Live free or die." Since his father was then in hiding, fearful for his life, these acts of treachery were not looked upon with favor. His family was forced eventually to send him to the lay school which the Republic had set up in Grenoble. There he proved a brilliant student of mathematics and used this talent as an excuse to get away from Grenoble, which he hated, to the Paris of which he had dreamed. On his way to the capital he heard that Napoleon had overthrown the Directory and proclaimed himself Consul of the Republic.

Beyle did not enter the Ecole Polytéchnique as he had planned; instead, thanks to an influential family connection, he was soon in the thick of the Napoleonic adventure. At seventeen he was certainly the most completely untrained lieutenant of dragoons who crossed the St. Bernard Pass into Italy with Napoleon's liberating army; at twenty-five he was Napoleon's satrap in the small German state of Brunswick; as an important staff member of the quartermaster corps he saw dozens of great battles and was on hand to see the all-conquering Emperor enter both Berlin and Moscow. His career from 1800 to 1814, when, as he sadly recorded, "I fell with Napoleon," was one of vigorous activity and significant achievement.

Napoleon Bonaparte was the key figure in the life of Henri Beyle and in the life of the hero of each of his two novels. It may be worth reminding ourselves, therefore, of the impact of this surcharged figure on the young men who served him. The Revolution had swept away a reactionary dictatorship of privilege which used every means to oppress the masses and secure its own position. But the Revolution brought its own terror and confusion, out of which rose an obscure corporal who in a few months transformed the buffeted, humiliated outcast of Europe. The stored energies which the Allies had managed to contain for a decade exploded over all Europe, and to be a Frenchman was to be a ruler of the world. France for centuries had been controlled by the elderly and the reactionary. Napoleon believed in youth and in talent, and he did not care where they came from. For the first time a young man could make his way on his merits alone—all the way to the top. A cooper's son, in a few breath-taking years, became marshal, duke, and prince. And any peasant's son could dream of becoming a general, an ambassador, or, like Henri Beyle, a commissary of war. The effect of this policy was to electrify the young men of France who rushed to take part in Napoleon's great adventures and in the golden splendor of the brilliant court he created.

But when Napoleon fell, the great experiment collapsed utterly. The Bourbons rode back into Paris and with the help of their allies set up a regime even more reactionary than that of Louis XIV and his successors. The standard apparatus for crushing freedom of thought and action descended upon the country once again. The brilliant careers that had been open under Napoleon to young men of spirit and intellect were wiped out. France settled back into stolid conformity to the will of her despotic masters.

Henri Beyle could have made his peace with the new regime, as some of Napoleon's other administrators did. But he had no stomach for it, and no talent for keeping his thoughts to himself. So, after a period of self-imposed exile in Milan (from which he was ejected as a dangerous liberal), he settled down quietly in Paris in narrow circumstances, and for ten years observed the world the Bourbons had made. He did a great deal of writing in this period, much of it ephemeral, and shortly before Charles X was dethroned by the Paris mobs, he began to write *The Red and the Black.*

The Henri Beyle for whom the early years of the Napoleonic era had been the dazzling fulfilment of a glorious dream must often have asked himself in the dreary days of the Restoration: "What in Heaven's name would have happened to me if I had been born twenty years later than I was, if I had reached maturity, full of driving ambition, at a time like the present when genius is throttled in the interests of absolute conformity to the will of a despotic government?" The answer in fictional terms is to be found in *The Red and the Black.* Its hero, Julien Sorel, might have been one of Napoleon's brilliant soldier-administrators, had he not had the misfortune to be born too late.

Julien not only begins life at the wrong time; he begins it without even the modest advantages of a Henri Beyle. His father is a sordid, shrewd, money-grabbing peasant, owner of a sawmill in the provincial town of Verrières (clearly a thinly disguised Grenoble). His mother, like Beyle's, died when he was a child. A slender, handsome young man at the age of eighteen, he is suddenly plucked from his father's sawmill and installed as tutor to the children of the town's mayor. This distinction Julien owes to his extraordinary memory—he knows every book of the New Testament by heart in Latin—and the recommendation of an old Jansenist priest with whom he has studied when his services were not required at the sawmill.

Though his knowledge of the practical world is infinitesimal at this point, Julien has already recognized the course that his life must take if his intense ambition, which he does everything possible to conceal, is to be served. Influenced by a retired army surgeon who lived for a while with his family, Julien has become a passionate Bonapartist. Oppressed by the cruelty of his father and his loutish brothers, he sees Napoleon with the eyes of the idealistic young men of a quarter century before, and his consuming desire is to perform vast fictive heroisms on a Napoleonic battlefield. But for Julien no such career is possible. The gods of the Restoration have restored the old ways. Army commissions go only to the sons of the aristocracy. A man's merit has no effect on his advancement. For Julien, determined at all costs to get ahead, to climb out of the sewer that he feels he is in, there is only one course. Only one avenue of advancement is still open to the man without a name. "I must," he decides, "become a priest." And the means of his attaining advancement in the church must be hypocrisy, for his Bonapartist sentiments rule out any sympathy for a church so constituted as to be an effective instrument of oppression. Having made his decision, he goes to study with the Abbé Chélan and learns his Vulgate by heart.

If he is ambitious, Julien is also proud with the fierce pride of the man who knows he deserves far more than he is accorded. In the negotiations with M. de Renal, the mayor, whose children Julien is to tutor, Julien's father is interested only in how much his son's salary will be; Julien is interested only in eating with the family rather than with the servants. Pride and ambition—these are the ruling passions in Julien's life. Hypocrisy in public and ruthless private adherence to his own conception of what he owes himself—these are the prevailing modes of his behavior. With them Julien marches forth to conquer the world.

Stendhal's study of the impact of this vigorous, sometimes ruthless energy on the sterile mediocrity of the world in which it must expend itself is full of subtlety and intricate detail. Here I can hope only to suggest something of the nature of this impact by looking briefly at the central action of each volume of *The Red and the Black*.

The situation I have described is, of course, latent with tragedy. The forces against which the hero must contend are too strong. And in the end he does die, his potential unfulfilled. But the tragic ending is not—as in *King Lear* or *Macbeth*—the inevitable consequence of a developing series of events. There is no terror here, and little pity. The hero's death is, in fact, the consequence of a curious and not altogether believable alteration in his view of himself. It is almost as if he has reached a state of complete emotional collapse. And when he is offered the opportunity to escape death, he deliberately and disdainfully refuses it. He does not blame himself for anything he has done, but he simply cannot go on. The world has squeezed him dry.

I labor this point because I want to suggest that *The Red and the Black*, like *The Charterhouse of Parma*, is essentially a comedy, that in the field of the novel it occupies a position much the same as that of *The Misanthrope* in the drama and that its basic techniques Stendhal had learned from Molière. As a young man he had been an ardent student of Molière, and for years his ambition was to be Molière's successor. Only after a multitude of attempts did he resign himself to the fact that he could not write for the stage. But he knew Molière's works inside out, and he shared his humane, detached, ironic view of mankind. His books, it seems to me, are in essential respects the equivalent in the novel of Molière's comic masterpieces.

Even the plot of *The Red and the Black* is reminiscent of *The Misanthrope*—each is the story of an intensely serious young man, utterly devoid of humor, who strives to reach a goal embedded in a society whose chief characteristic is its shallowness. But the protagonist cannot reach the goal. Like the dreamer of a bad dream, he sees the desire of his heart ahead of him, but no matter how hard he tries, he cannot bring it any closer. He tries to push aside the petty world without compromising his essential integrity. But in each instance the world wins, the protagonist retires from the field.

Molière's biographers tell us that there is much of Molière in Alceste, the misanthrope; the play has been somewhat misleadingly referred to as his *Hamlet*. There is much of Henri Beyle in Julien Sorel; no doubt someone has called *The Red and the Black* his *Hamlet*. All of which is simply to say that each work may be autobiographical in part and each is a serious comedy.

Whether a work is comic or tragic depends, of course, not on the subject matter or even the plot, but on the way subject matter and plot are handled. And at the risk of oversimplifying, I should suggest that essentially the job of the writer of tragedy is to involve the reader or audience as deeply as possible in the exaltation and the despair of his characters, whereas the job of the writer of comedy is to keep the reader—by every means at his disposal

—*from* becoming emotionally involved with his protagonist. He strives to
keep the reader detached (emotionally, not intellectually) from the characters. The characteristic observation point for the comic writer is the area
of the moon, from which he may look down on the world and see man
for the weak, petty creature that he is. Puck, that extra-human sprite out
of a midsummer night's dream, sees man in the true comic perspective.
"Lord," he says, "what fools these mortals be!" To a writer like Molière
or Stendhal who achieves comic detachment from his material, all of mankind's petty projects are folly, irony is everywhere. And the more seriously
an individual takes himself, the more ludicrous he is likely to seem, no
matter how worthy his aims.

Julien Sorel takes himself very seriously indeed, but no more seriously
than Alceste. The young Stendhal had also taken himself most seriously.
But his journals and his letters clearly indicate that even as a young man,
and more pronouncedly as he grew older, he was able to act and at the same
time to stand outside his actions, seeing the sorry part he was playing but
feeling within himself the necessity to play it anyway. Thus Julien can have
much of Henri Beyle in him, even be an idealized version of his creator,
and still be essentially a comic figure. Not all readers, to be sure, see him
as comic. Their reaction is understandable, for Julien is a vital, vivid, and
in most respects admirable individual with whom we are strongly tempted
to identify ourselves, especially because he fights valiantly against the forces
of intellectual and spiritual degradation. Many of us are similarly tempted
to identify ourselves with the plain-spoken Alceste in his battle with the
fops who surround Célimene. But if we are to identify ourselves with either
of these figures, as we do with Othello or King Lear, we must ignore the
total context in which he is presented. An unclouded view of this context—
which is to say a mature reading of the works—will place Alceste and Julien
in proper perspective as comic figures in a comic setting.

Let me illustrate briefly what I have in mind, as far as Julien is concerned, by looking at one critical action from each part of the novel. No
dramatic scene, except perhaps the death of a hero, may be more breath-
takingly serious, more beautiful, more romantic than that which unites a
truly loving pair in the face of opposition. One thinks of the tenderness
and the intense seriousness with which Shakespeare handles the scene in
which Romeo climbs the balcony to visit his stolen bride and the even
more touching scene in which the lark sings and Juliet forces herself to
send her husband away. Julien Sorel is Romeo, at different times, to two
Juliets. To each he comes in the dead of night; from each he departs only
when night's candles are burned out. A brief examination of the circumstances leading to what might be the most romantic of moments will perhaps suggest something of the quality of Stendhal's treatment of his hero.

After he is settled in the house of the mayor of Verrières, whom he despises—and quite rightly—as a petty time-server, Julien is much in the company of the mayor's young, attractive, and thoroughly innocent wife. But he has no romantic interest in her at all; indeed he sees her as an enemy, an ally of her husband. One day as he is sitting with Mme. de Renal, he happens, while gesticulating in an animated conversation, accidentally to place his hand on hers. Instinctively she withdraws her hand and thereby sets off a curious chain of circumstances. The effect on Julien is described by Stendhal as follows: "This hand was very quickly withdrawn; but Julien felt it his *duty* to manage things so that this hand should not be withdrawn when he touched it. The idea of a duty to be carried out, and of making himself ridiculous or rather being made to feel his inferiority if he failed, banished at once every thought of pleasure from his heart." The next morning, we learn, this solemn student of Napoleon's tactics takes "stock of her as of an enemy he had to fight"; and he determines to attack in the evening when, as is their custom, he and Mme. de Renal and her friend Mme. Derville will be sitting on the terrace. When the time comes, he spends a miserable hour trying to summon up his courage to do his duty. He can't. Finally, "indignant with his own cowardice," he says to himself: "The moment ten o'clock strikes, I'll carry [it] out, or else I'll go upstairs and blow my brains out." At the final stroke of the bell, he seizes the prize, she pulls it away, he grasps it again, and she allows it to remain. "His heart was overflowing with happiness," Stendhal tells us, "not from any love for Madame de Renal, but because a frightful state of torment was at an end. He had done his *duty*, and an *heroic duty*, too." Filled with joy he locks himself in his room and abandons himself. To thinking about his loved one? Not at all. He abandons himself to reading Napoleon's memoirs.

But his happiness does not last long. A few days later, Mme. de Renal, afraid Julien may leave to take another post, shows some signs of innocent affection for him. As a result, he abruptly decides: "I owe it to myself to become her lover." On the same evening, Mme. de Renal, who is beginning to suspect that she is in some danger of finding affection turn to love, also comes to a decision: "I'll never grant Julien any favours. We'll go on living in the future as we have been this month." This somewhat naive decision is hardly unexpected, for Stendhal has made clear that she is a thoroughly good woman, who has "never in her life experienced anything in the least like love" and (as we are told twice in the same words) has "had not the slightest experience of life."

What follows Julien's decision is one of the more grotesque seductions in literature. On the basis of a story or two he has heard from a friend and "the little he had read of love in the Bible" he draws up, after the Napoleonic model, "a closely detailed plan of campaign" and then proceeds to set it down in writing. The next day he inexpertly kisses her in broad daylight "as she is going through a doorway." She is shocked and scolds him for his imprudence. The following evening he sits down beside her and whispers without preamble, "Madame, tonight at two I will come to your room. There's something I must say to you." Julien, we are then told, "was trembling lest his request be granted." Mme. de Renal is thoroughly indignant. "You ought to be ashamed," she says. But that night, when two o'clock finally strikes, we are treated to a picture of the Lover, "keeping his idea of a *duty to himself* unceasingly before his eyes" lest he turn and run, his knees knocking so much that he has to lean against the wall to steady himself, tiptoeing, shoes in hand, down the hall. It is all in the best comic tradition. He even makes a "frightful noise" as he opens his lady's door.

From this richly comic assault there develops gradually, and not without many a misunderstanding and mishap, a strong bond of love between the two. Stendhal, drawing on the experience of his own love affairs—of which there were several—traces the steps in the lover's progress with keen psychological insight. Mme. de Renal develops into a human being of warmth and sincerity. Julien is thawed so that he becomes at times almost a genuine Romeo. But he can be genuine only as long as he is alone with Mme. de Renal. As soon as he touches the world outside her home, or it invades their private world, Julien becomes once again his curmudgeonish, cantankerous self. He learns much from love, but his basic motivations remain unchanged. So does his basic role. The reader may get the impression at times that Julien's role will no longer continue to be comic. If so, Stendhal sets him straight at the conclusion of the first part of the novel. Julien has been forced to leave Verrières because of the husband's suspicions. After several months in a seminary, he returns in the dead of night to see the woman he loves. The final interview takes place in Mme. de Renal's room, to which Julien has climbed, like Romeo, up a ladder. They are interrupted by the jealous husband, who roars to his wife to open her locked door. Julien leaps out the window, and Part I ends with our Napoleonic hero racing across the fields stark naked, clutching his clothes to him, while a valet and a gardener blast away with ineffective buckshot.

This is the noisily comic end of the first great adventure—in the world of the petty bourgeoisie. The second is in the world of the aristocracy, but the results are no more satisfactory. Because he impresses the head of the seminary, Julien one day finds himself private secretary to the Marquis de la Mole, a shrewd, headstrong but somewhat vacillating leader of the ultra-royalists, who is said to be in line for one of the highest posts in the government. To the salon of the Marquis come the most distinguished men of Charles X's court. As the Marquis's secretary, Julien is often present.

In his black habit, faintly reminiscent of Hamlet in the corrupt Danish court, he wanders around the room, listening. Though there are distinguished—even brilliant—individuals present, he finds the conversation stale, empty, mechanical. He senses that everyone is being very careful about what he says. The only person who interests the young secretary is a Spaniard, Count Altamira, who started a revolution in his own country, found he could not be ruthless enough to carry it through, escaped to France, and now waits patiently while the French government makes up its mind— as it inevitably will, we learn—to hand him over to the Spanish king for execution. With Altamira only, Julien partially drops the mask of hypocrisy which he has brought with him from the provinces. For Altamira differs from the others—both the mature returned émigrés and the brave and cultured young suitors of the Marquis's daughter: he can speak his mind and has proved that he can act on his convictions. It is when we compare him with the others that we realize why the evenings are so deadly at the Marquis de la Mole's. There no one can speak of any of the things that interest him. As under any totalitarian regime, the expression of genuine ideas has become dangerous. Court spies are everywhere, and no remark is safe which contains anything that can possibly be construed as disloyal to the established government. So one avoids ideas and sticks to platitudes and gossip. In the Hotel de la Mole there is no energy, no life—except in the Marquis's daughter, Mathilde.

Like Julien, Mathilde de la Mole is an outsider in her father's salon. A girl of great energy, wit, and force of character, she easily dominates the social group to which she belongs. Her suitors find her a bit queer, but her beauty, her wealth, and her father's position outweigh their reservations. For her part, she is bored to death with their want of character and with what she calls a "degenerate and tedious age" in which chance and the unexpected have ceased to exist. So bored is she that she deliberately writes indiscreet letters to her suitors in a desperate attempt to stir up some excitement and turns to the past for an image of life which will satisfy her vision of what the world should be. As Julien looks back with longing to the Napoleonic era, Mathilde looks back to a much earlier era of vigor and energy. Her Golden Age is the court of Henry III, one of whose boldest spirits was her ancestor, Boniface de la Mole, "the handsomest young man of his age." Boniface made love to no less a personage than Queen Marguerite of Navarre, participated in all manner of derring-do, and, betrayed by his friends, was beheaded on April 30, 1574. Boniface had all of the heroic qualities that Mathilde seeks—and does not find—in the young men who wish to marry her. In his memory she puts on mourning each April 30.

Clearly Mlle. de la Mole and Julien Sorel have much in common; since they alone in this society have character, energy, and ideals, they inevitably interest each other. And so, while Julien wears his mask of hypocrisy in public, becomes the Marquis's most trusted employee, wins a coveted cross of honor, carries a memorized secret message from a council of the Ultra-Royalists to a high personage in the English government, and takes over his mentor's financial affairs—he conducts a most curious semi-military engagement with Mlle. de la Mole.

One might perhaps expect these two outsiders to join forces against the world. But this is not easily accomplished, for Julien is a peasant's son, Mathilde is the daughter of an ancient and noble house. In an age when birth once again is everything, neither can forget these facts. Even without the bar of origin, these two are perhaps too much alike for easy companionship. Each is inordinately proud—quick to resent the least slight. Each is full of restless energy and is frustrated because that energy has no adequate outlet. The mercury on the emotional thermometer of each reaches to both extremes and is constantly leaping from one level to another. Since the level on the two thermometers is seldom the same, Julien and Mathilde constantly irritate each other and only rarely reach any kind of understanding. There is a constant attraction, yet a constant war between them which cannot be resolved without the submission of one or the other. And to neither has the thought of submission ever occurred. For these two young people, their private war is profoundly serious. It has all the intensity of a D. H. Lawrence love affair—though the quality is somewhat different. But despite this intensity, Stendhal's treatment of their activities keeps reminding us that the frustration of living in an alien world has stretched their nerves so taut, made each so much the servant of hair-triggered pride, that to the objective observer their actions must seem profoundly comic.

As an example, we may look briefly at the scenes which lead up to Mathilde's giving herself to Julien. The two have been sparring, more or less viciously, for some months. Whenever Mathilde gives him a warm glance, Julien is immediately suspicious. "The reader," Stendhal says at one point, "is but little acquainted with [Julien's] character if he has not already seen the sombre, chilly expression on his face in response to Mathilde's [warm] glances. A bitter irony repulsed the assurances of friendship which [she], astonished by his conduct, ventured to risk on two or three occasions." And whenever Julien is inclined to be friendly, she finds her father's peasant secretary too familiar and tramples on his pride. Finally, exhausted by the struggle, he plans to slip out of town to recuperate. But she finds out. Her first reaction is to tell him he *must* not go—which, of course, offends him. (He recalls that "Louis XV, too, at the point of death, had been deeply vexed by the word *must*, clumsily used by his chief physician, and Louis XV was no upstart.") Mathilde, recognizing her error, follows the order with a note which is a simple declaration of love. At first

Julien is delighted. He puts off his trip. Then he begins to worry. Is it a device of the lady and her father to trap him into betraying himself? (This is the world of Charles X still.) He sends her an enigmatic reply and plans to circumvent the potential snare. She writes again. He threatens a second time to leave town. Then he receives a curious and characteristic note. "The moment one o'clock strikes, see that you are in the garden. Take the gardener's long ladder; put it up against my window and climb up to my room. There is a moon tonight; but that doesn't matter." To Julien the moon profoundly matters. It seems to him quite clear that Mathilde is setting up a foolproof ambush. Her brother's room is above hers; the garden is full of bushes and trees behind which an army of servants with firearms may be hidden. And at one o'clock, Julien will be halfway up the ladder in the bright moonlight.

What happens? He decides that he owes it to himself to go. Armed to the teeth, pistol in hand, he follows her instructions. As we have seen, he has used a ladder before. Up he goes—and steps lightly into the lady's room.

"So you're here, sir!" she says. And thus begins what should be the tenderest of love scenes. But it is everything else. Mathilde has tested her hero and has found his courage worthy of a successor to the heroic Boniface de la Mole; but when she arranged the test, we discover, she had never really counted on Julien's passing it. Now she is horrified by what she has let herself in for: her upbringing has been strict and in her temperament there is nothing of the wanton. She is further annoyed by a hint that Julien may consider himself her master. Above all, she is incredulous at her own folly. For his part, Julien "was amazed at his lack of happiness." But each is now committed, and in a scene drenched with irony, these two unwilling lovers prod themselves to do what they consider their duty to themselves and to each other. "To tell the truth," Stendhal comments dryly, "their transports were somewhat forced. Passionate love was still rather more of a model they were imitating than the real thing."

This scene is only the beginning of a stormy romance, which ends finally in Mathilde's capitulation. But I hope that my account of it suggests the consistently detached, ironic tone of this complex and detailed study of the energetic idealist in a despotic society. Certain conclusions seem inescapable. Julien, who believes implicitly in the Napoleonic ideal of vigorous achievement on a heroic scale and who is determined at all costs to fulfil his ambition, is forced from the start to adopt a mask. He has no choice. Should he at any time announce himself a Bonapartist, he would immediately find himself in prison. One of the conditions of living, for him, is that he be a hypocrite; and this condition, in turn, though *he* does not know it, makes it impossible for him to achieve greatly.

As an emotional and intellectual recompense for the hypocrisy which is forced upon him, Julien develops an exaggerated conception of his duty to himself, a passionate pride which is a constant affront to those who think of themselves as his betters. And if it attracts women like Mme. de Renal and Mathilde, it makes the road to the highest form of love—"passion-love" Stendhal calls it in his essay *On Love*—a very rocky one indeed. To Stendhal, passion-love, of which only truly superior people are capable, is perhaps the supreme experience of life. For Julien, weighed down by his mask and his swollen pride, passion-love is impossible. Only after he has shot Mme. de Renal—an act which he thinks of as retaliation for the letter which destroys his plan to marry Mathilde but really seems to be an act of love—only after he has condemned himself to death and removed the need both for hypocrisy and pride, is he capable of the highest form of love. But then it is too late.

If we ask what impression this dedicated seeker after Napoleonic greatness has made on the world, we are forced to conclude that it is very slight indeed. Love for him has transformed the cardboard doll who was known as Mme. de Renal into a passionate, mature woman—but she has been destroyed in the process. He has caused a rare commotion in a nobleman's family and left its jewel tarnished. But that is not a distinguished record for a protegé of Napoleon. Stendhal's answer, I'm afraid, is that the man of energy and ideals has no real place in and can have no real effect on a world living under despotism. We feel about Julien, as we do about Alceste, a sadness that so much good should be wasted, but we recognize nonetheless that in the context in which he is placed, his single-minded devotion to an ideal is a form of madness which can only end in disaster. But the disaster is seen as ironic rather than tragic. Irony follows Julien even to the grave. He has directed that he should be buried in an isolated, romantic cave on a mountain peak where in happier days he had gone to think his deepest thoughts. There alone, he had felt that he could drop all masks and be himself. He is buried there; but, Stendhal tells us, "Mathilde's loving care had this rude cave adorned with marbles sculptured at great cost in Italy."

To Henri Beyle, who lived much of his life under the surveillance of Metternich's secret agents, the essential ingredient of life was the ability to realize one's potential. He had seen in the days of the Great Adventure the effect of a gust of freedom in developing the potential of a whole nation and of millions of individual Frenchmen. In later life he observed at first hand the numbing effects of totalitarian government, which crushed its foes and made man's life a pathetic travesty of what it might have been.

But Stendhal never conceived that the world would continue to be ruled by despots. The comic artist is always an idealist. In his mind's eye shines a vision of life as it *could* be. Henri Beyle had seen what could be accomplished by the energetic idealist in a different world from the one he studies in his novels. And he believed that mankind, having known freedom, could not long be held in bondage, and that the time would again come when a man of character would be able to live with dignity and honor. No doubt this faith, which is implicit in everything he wrote, has much to do with the fact that in the great lottery of fame he did indeed hold a winning number.

UNDERGROUND MAN AND SAINT IN DOSTOEVSKI

To us now the figure of Dostoevski stands astride the nineteenth century. That century, however, had only a hazy knowledge of his greatness, although it did take three separate opportunities to sing his praises, once when he was very young, once in middle life, once when he was an old man. For the rest of the time, the world, as the populace did with the returned Christ in Ivan Karamazov's parable in *The Brothers Karamazov*, saw him, knew him for what he was, and averted its gaze. No one of his time walked more completely "in disgrace with Fortune and men's eyes"—trained for a profession he despised; sentenced to death for belonging to a secret, revolutionary society; exiled upon reprieve for the ten best years of his life; married most unhappily; burdened with debt his life long; subject to frequently recurring, and shattering, epileptic fits; seized of a mania for gambling that reduced him from mere poverty to utter destitution; arrogant and self-debased by turns; possessed of brief flights of happiness succeeded by terrible periods of despair; discourteous, harsh, irresponsible, loud, insulting, often hateful. It is no wonder his century averted its gaze, you say. We should avert our gaze too. Such a man deserved neglect, and worse. The world had every right to stand in judgment on him.

But such was not the essential relationship between his world and him. When I said he stands astride his century, I meant first of all in time, for the years of his life numbered roughly thirty before the middle of the century and thirty after; and secondly, like Gulliver among the Lilliputians, or perhaps better Zeus among the mortals, he watched his contemporaries go through their petty paces and nimble acrobatics while they hugged to their breast their fondest shibboleths, their cherished slogans, their half-formed ideas, their pious hypocrisies, their carefully shielded vices. In the full tide of Victorian prosperity and optimism, when Tennyson was composing *The Idylls of the King*, that tribute to fair and virtuous England, and Browning was just about to write the optimistic *Rabbi Ben Ezra*, Dostoevski stood on a corner in London, seeing pitilessly, unflinchingly his version of this great Victorian world:

> In London . . . every Saturday night half a million workers, men and women, with their children, spill into the streets like a flood . . . eating and drinking like beasts, to last, one would think, the whole week. . . . All seem to be set on getting dead drunk as quickly as possible. Wives are no better than their men and get drunk with them; the children run about and crawl among them. . . .
>
> Here you are no longer aware even of people, but of an insensible human mass, a general loss of consciousness, systematic, resigned. . . .

Presumably: "Grow old along with me, the best bender is yet to be." But if his glance was more microscopically piercing than his contemporaries', it was also more inclusive; and his judgment of his world was general and far-reaching.

A phrase Dostoevski uses in *The Diary of a Writer*, turned slightly, will, I hope, be helpful in describing this larger criticism of his century. In *The Diary* he discusses the conformity of many artists of his day who are following a school or a group in their painting, instead of, as he says, "revealing themselves in images that are peculiarly their own." These artists he refers to as "artists in uniform." It is clear here that he is thinking of intellectual conformity and, that being so, I should like to change Dostoevski's phrase, which I like much better than my own, but to change it for clarity's sake to "the artist's mind in uniform."

The artist's mind in uniform, the moralist's mind in uniform, the social reformer's mind in uniform, the romanticist's mind in uniform. Mind in uniform in general and in all its aspects: that is, mind committed, before experience teaches it, to a theory or idea, a belief or program or dream by which it tries to live. That is the basic point of attack in Dostoevski.

Let us look at some of the various types of mind in uniform that Dostoevski analyzes. A fundamental one is that of romanticism, which had flowered, had almost overrun the house, at the turn of the nineteenth century. The romanticist's image of true love Dostoevski deals with early in his career. In a short story *White Nights*, a young girl is wooed by a lonely young man who has sympathetically heard her story of love unrequited and has in turn poured out to her his own years of bitter loneliness, with such effect that she cries out: "I don't love him [her former lover], because I can only love what is generous, what is understanding, what is honorable...," characteristics possessed in abundance by the young man. But within half an hour of this earnestly spoken, sincere speech, she throws herself into the arms of her former lover and goes off with him. "Generous, understanding, honorable," deserving of reward and fulfilment (though after many trials)—these characteristics of the true lover in Schiller, in Scott, in Dickens, in Thackeray, are not even relevant in Dostoevski. Substitute the picture of Dmitri Karamazov, who in a jealous rage inspired by his frightening love knocks his father to the floor and kicks him in the face.

Or consider another aspect of romanticism, the Byronic hero, noble or satanic, who paraded himself before the world, aloof, handsome, suffering with secret knowledge that set him apart, a monster of ego and self-concern. The Dostoevskian gallery is well stocked with such as he, Stavrogin, the dark unknown hero of *The Possessed*, most prominently, but none more clearly than Katerina in *The Brothers Karamazov*, who loves Ivan Karamazov and is beloved by him but determines to give her hand in marriage to Dmitri, to sacrifice herself her whole life to reform him—to save him, as she sees it. "You need [Dmitri]," says Ivan to her, "so as to contemplate continually your heroic fidelity and to reproach him for infidelity. And it all comes from pride." The Byronic pose of suffering and sacrifice was not confined to Byron or to any one man. It infected the young Tennyson and Disraeli, Stavrogin and Dmitri Karamazov and Katerina and the hearts of countless unknowns, men and women, throughout nineteenth-century Europe.

But after all, the romantic mind in uniform is only one concern of Dostoevski. The social reformer's mind in uniform is just as bad, and among intellectuals even more prevalent. We would expect from what I have said of Dostoevski's life that he would strongly sympathize with social reformers, perhaps even revolutionary groups. After all, he himself was a member of a secret society, and for his membership and activity (which was innocent enough) he was sentenced to be shot and later exiled from Russia for ten years. But we know that he was only a half-serious member of the group and that he later came to regard his exile as a blessing because, for one thing, it saved him from being trapped in a "uniform" he came to despise. In *The Possessed* he pictures the existence of such a reform and revolutionary group, analyzing pitilessly what becomes of the members who are drawn to the group by theories of the betterment of the lower classes, are victimized by their unscrupulous leader, and are finally led (or *made* would perhaps be a much better word) to commit murder in order to tie the members irrevocably in guilt to their leader. More familiar, perhaps, would be the figure of Lebeziatnikov, that minor character in *Crime and Punishment*, who lives with Luzhin and who is scorned by the author for his pseudo-intellectuality. He spouts the clichés of the nineteenth-century revolutionary: environment is everything, man by himself is nothing; everything that is useful to mankind is honorable; everything possible must be done to free woman from such prejudices as marriage; chastity and feminine modesty are useless in themselves and mere survivals from the past. This last is rendered preposterous in the context of the novel because Lebeziatnikov uses Sonia, the unfortunate prostitute of the story, as his model, praising her actions because they are, in his words, "a forceful and personal protest against our present organization of society"—certainly the furthest thought from Sonia's mind. When he then expresses his admiration for her emancipation and the hope that she will choose to give herself to him, Luzhin cuts him short with: "If I were you I'd give her some present. I bet you never thought of that." In this ridiculous figure, Dostoevski personifies the social revolutionary who parrots ideals and mouths theories and understands nothing of human nature, others' or his own.

With both of these criticisms we can live fairly comfortably. The diseases belong primarily (at least in the form Dostoevski describes them) to the nineteenth century. And with the help of eighty years' hindsight we smile indulgently. But the attack has only begun, and from the next blows we are left reeling. The moralist's, the social scientist's, the rationalist's mind in uniform, all come under the steely eye of Dostoevski. In one work in particular the attack is frontal and brutal; this work is *Notes from the Underground*, and I should like to examine it for a few minutes at close range.

The narrator lives alone in a tiny room—his underground, as he calls it—just like a mouse in the wall. Here he remains wrapped in his own thoughts and ideas. He occasionally goes forth among his fellow men but always retires gladly to his underground world, there to brood about himself and the people he has just met. He feels himself to be acutely conscious and sensitive, and this sensitivity produces in him strange reactions to events and ideas. For example, he is always being insulted by insensitive people, "having his face slapped," as he puts it; but he does not take revenge on these people, although he contemplates it and broods about it. Instead he goes on having his face slapped by plain, insensitive men of action; "all that is left for the mouse to do," he says, "is to dismiss [each insult] with a disdainful wave of its little paw and with a smile of simulated contempt, in which it does not believe itself, to scurry back ingloriously into its hole," and there plot its revenge.

But the more he thinks about the latest insult or any insult, the more the thought of revenge evaporates. He is a supersensitive man, his opponent a man of action; each performs as nature has directed him to. "One look and the object [revenge] disappears into thin air," he says; "your reasons evaporate, there is no guilty man, the injury is no longer an injury but just fate . . . and consequently," he winds up, "there is only one solution left, namely knocking your head against the wall as hard as you can." After which his pain changes gradually into a sort of shameful, damnable sweetness and finally into real, positive delight.

If such a strange man exists, of what importance is he? On his own evidence he is a mouse and not to be taken seriously. He must be just a joke Dostoevski is playing on us. But no, far from it; for Dostoevski sets his mouse-man against the whole modern world. At this point in the story, the narrator, the mouse-man, shifts his ground. He speaks in more general terms of philosophers and prophets who look with satisfaction upon the scientific and material success of man and with eagerness upon his approaching triumph not only over nature but over himself. The laws of nature in man will be discovered, they say, and then he will act according to his own best interests, and in this Crystal Palace (or *Brave New World*) of the future, man will live in peace and prosperity and virtue and happiness. But the narrator denies this conclusion, denies it with all the force at his command. The history of the world suggests that man does not act in his own interest; furthermore, the values that these philosophers list leave out the most important one—free choice; and to preserve this one value man will sacrifice all the others. Even if reason penetrated all the laws of man's behavior, man would go to any length—plan destruction and chaos, utter a curse upon the world, if necessary go purposely mad—in order to maintain the right to desire for himself the stupid act in preference to the act that nature's laws and the experts on nature's laws set down as good for him. "For reason is only reason," he says, "while volition is a manifestation of the whole of life. . . , of the whole of life, including reason with all its concomitant head-scratchings."

Why, then, does the supersensitive mouse-man, humiliated, without courage, without a desire for revenge, creep into his underground hole and beat his head futilely against the wall, finding pleasure in the pain? He does so because, since nature has cast him in this insignificant mold, he has no other way of expressing his will, of showing that he is after all a man capable of free choice and not a victim of inscrutable and immutable laws. The most helpless, the most cowardly, the most futile of men will exert his will even if it means bringing the world down around his ears, even if it means crime, or evil, or debasement. Man will not accept nature's laws; he will not serve. In this enormous vision the Crystal Palace, as Dostoevski calls it, constructed of scientific determinism and materialism, social panaceas and reforms, all the social sciences put together—the Crystal Palace of the future lists and crumbles before puny, vile, debased, mud-wallowing, but freely choosing man.

With the ideals of romanticism, the vision of Utopian reform, the prospect of scientific improvement damned and swept away, what then remains? The world, we feel, surely must return to chaos and old night. But Dostoevski, having cleared the ground, would work to see what is left, to determine what reality, if any, remains. In *Crime and Punishment* he gives us a fictional picture of the emergence of the underground man and the possibilities that exist for his salvation.

Consider first, in Raskolnikov, the analysis of the underground man. Raskolnikov commits murder, plans it all out beforehand, justifies the specific case on the grounds that a young, desperately needy student, sensitive to all that is fine in life, capable of great achievement, intelligent far beyond the average, has more right to live, to use the money in the old woman's possession, than she has, old and useless, crabbed and stupid as she is. And he justifies such an action in general on the grounds that there is a special class of men (Napoleon is the prototype in his mind) for whom moral laws do not apply, who actually by transgressing moral laws may bring a new achievement, a new word, as he puts it, to man; and the contribution would more than justify the immorality.

But when he commits the murders, how diffetently he behaves! The money he never uses, hiding it in fear of its being discovered. He falls into a terrible fever and delirium from which he does not fully recover for weeks. On many occasions he confesses his crime, or virtually does so, daring his listeners to believe him, wanting them to know he has committed the murders. Is this the way for the theoretician to act? How can the fine-spun theories stand up under such behavior? They of course do not. When to the woman he loves he explains each of these theories as the motives for his crime, he sees the falseness of them, the rationalization in them, the mind-in-uniform quality of each of them, and he sees that they do not apply. They are fabricated motives. The real motive lies elsewhere. The real motive is the motive of the underground mouse-man:

> I sat in my room like a spider. Ah, how I hated that garret! And
> yet I wouldn't go out of it! I wouldn't on purpose! I didn't go out
> for days together, and I wouldn't work, I wouldn't even eat, I just
> lay there doing nothing. If [the maid] brought me anything, I ate
> it, if she didn't I went all day without; I wouldn't ask, on purpose,
> for sulkiness! I ought to have studied, but I sold all my books . . .
> I preferred lying still and thinking. And I kept thinking . . . I had to
> endure all the agony of the battle of ideas, Sonia, and I longed to
> throw it off: I wanted to murder without casuistry, to murder for
> my own sake, for myself alone! I didn't want to lie about it even
> to myself. It wasn't to [get the money and] to help my mother I
> did the murder—that's nonsense—I didn't do the murder to gain
> wealth and power and to become a benefactor of mankind. Non-

sense! I simply did it; I did the murder for myself, for myself alone
. . . . I wanted to find out then and quickly whether I was a louse
like everybody else or a man.

The mouse-louse-man from the underground. Man's will makes mincemeat
of his reason, turns the world upside down, tears down the oldest and
most stable moral laws of man. Murder is worse than beating one's head
against the wall, but the cause, the motive, is the same. What chance have
reason and law and order against the will, the desire, the passion of man?
None at all.

But this is not all that must be said about Raskolnikov. For this is
only the discovery by him of what he is; the novel tells us further what
happens to him after he has discovered what he is. What happens to him
can be better understood if we consider for a little what happens to two
other characters in *Crime and Punishment*: Marmeladov and Svidrigailov.
They are both mouse-men, subject to their own desires and wills in spite
of everything that would seem to be good for them and those they love.
Marmelodov is the easier to grasp.

He is a drunkard, unable to resist his alcoholism no matter what—his wife
dying of consumption, her small children by a previous marriage cold and
hungry, his daughter driven to prostitution. Trying for the last time to pick
up the pieces of his life, he gets himself a job and is treated on his first pay-
day like a king by his wife and daughter and the little ones; then in the middle of the night, he steals the money (he feels that he is stealing it) and goes
off on a five-day drunk, winding it up by calling on his daughter to take
her latest and last earnings for a final round of the taverns before he goes
home. Utter shame and disgrace and self-abasement seize him. Neither
intellectual nor theoretician, he nevertheless sees his shame perfectly clearly
and suffers terribly for it, and has for just a moment a vision of his salvation born of his ignoble behavior, his shame, and his suffering. At the Last
Judgment, the Lord will say:

"Come forth ye, too! Come forth, all ye who are drunk!" And
we shall come forth without being ashamed, and we shall stand
before Him. And the wise men will say, and the learned men will
say, "Lord, why dost thou receive them?" And He will say unto
them, "I receive them, O wise men, I receive them, O learned men,
because not one of them ever thought himself worthy of it." And
He will stretch forth his arm to us, and we shall fall down before
Him and we shall weep. And we shall understand all. Yes, we shall
understand all—and all will understand, and my wife, my wife,
will understand.

The last sentence is the significant one in this context. The man of
isolation, the man of awareness, the man of complete culpability, needs

understanding, trust, love. Marmeladov selects Raskolnikov as audience because Raskolnikov will give him a sympathetic hearing—an important consideration—but the understanding, the love, only Marmeladov's wife can give him. When she does not, when she is unable to, he is doomed to swift destruction.

Svidrigailov is a more complicated version of the same thing. In him, sensualism is the ruling passion, the dominant way in which he asserts his will, against good sense, against reputation, against the welfare of the women he has seduced, against the kind of life he himself would ideally like to lead. But the low life he lives he cannot give up. He too finds Raskolnikov a companion and a confessor for his crimes; and he seeks not only understanding but also companionship in crime with a murderer. He sees himself as lost, as bound irreparably to his passions, and he feels shame and loathing for his life.

Only one chance remains for him. One woman has fascinated him above all others, Raskolnikov's sister, Dunya. He loves her; if he can have her love, perhaps he will be saved. He traps her into meeting him in a locked room which no one has seen her enter and from which she cannot be heard. He himself does not know fully what his intentions are in thus meeting her. But she, when she discovers her situation, accuses him of intending to force her to submit to him. She draws a gun to defend herself but Svidrigailov, instead of being alarmed, welcomes this judgment on his whole lustful life. He invites her, almost commands her to shoot, and she does, twice: with one shot she grazes his ear; on the second the gun misfires. After this she drops the gun and Svidrigailov goes up to her.

He went up to Dunya and put his arm gently around her waist. She did not resist, but trembling violently, looked at him with eyes full of entreaty. He wanted to say something, but his lips twitched and he could not bring out a single word.

"Let me go," Dunya said in an imploring voice.

Svidrigailov shuddered: there was a strangely intimate note in her voice which was not there before.

"So you don't love me?" he asked softly.

Dunya shook her head.

"And—you can't? Never?" he whispered in despair.

"Never!" whispered Dunya.

For a moment a terrible, silent struggle was taking place in Svidrigailov's heart. He looked at her with an expression of unutterable anguish. Then suddenly he withdrew his arm, turned away, walked quickly to the window and stopped in front of it. . . .

"Here's the key! . . . . Take it and go at once!" . . . .

"At once! At once!"

There was evidently a terrible menace in that "at once," for

Dunya understood it and seizing the key, rushed to the door, un-
locked it quickly and ran out of the room.

Svidrigailov picks up the little gun, and the following morning after a
restless, nightmarish night, ends his life.

Raskolnikov faces a comparable decision, for it is said more than once
that his alternatives are Siberia or suicide. But Raskolnikov finds something
that neither of the other men could find: a special kind of love from woman.
He has decided that Sonia, Marmeladov's daughter, who has gone on the
streets to help her family survive, must be told his terrible secret, for he
has been strangely drawn to her pitiable plight and he sees in her a sympathetic suffering soul to whom he can speak freely. And when he tells her of
his crime, he encounters no righteousness, no condemnation, no moral
maxims, though she is deeply shocked at the information. Instead, her
reaction is one of profound sympathy and love: "Oh, what have you done
to yourself?" "Oh, I don't think there is any one in the world more unhappy than you are!" "What are we going to do now? Let's stay together,
together." The acceptance without judgment, without criticism, with complete love and understanding, makes salvation possible for Raskolnikov.
The kind of understanding, faith, and love Svidrigailov needs from Dunya
and Marmeladov needs from his wife, Sonia is able to give him.

And notice how the quality of love in Sonia fits in with Dostoevski's
criticisms of the mind in uniform. No stereotype of behavior or morality
motivates her love for Raskolnikov. Marmeladov's wife is filled with notions
of how he should behave, of the kind of life she used to lead and should
still lead, and she cannot accept him, cannot even see him, for what he is.
Nor can Dunya take Svidrigailov as he is; her idea of herself and of what
she expects of a husband is elevated and idealistic, and she consequently
must reject him.

Thus, what looks like a terrible indictment of all of modern life (for it
seems that the expression of man's will always takes an evil turn) is not
necessarily a prophecy of evil. The conventional romantic pattern of behavior in love won't do, Byronic egoism won't do, social reform, scientific
progress won't do; only love suffices, love that has as its first requirement
the acceptance of the loved one as he is.

Such love is helpful in turning man's generous impulses to good account, in enabling him to bear the suffering he must bear in order to be a
better person. But, as presented in *Crime and Punishment*, it is helpful only
to the individual, and a kindred spirit alone is able to offer this help. What
makes the problem difficult, as Dostoevski sees, is that there are many people
who need such love and cannot find it. Love between two individuals offers
hope to man, but shows its limitations quickly.

In novels written after *Crime and Punishment*, particularly *The Idiot* and *The Brothers Karamazov*, Dostoevski tries to find other grounds, other terms for salvation. In the time remaining, I should like to confine my attention to *The Brothers Karamazov*, Dostoevski's last and unquestionably his greatest novel. My approach, I am sorry to say, will probably be disappointing to those acquainted with the novel, for the great dramatic figures Dmitri and Ivan Karamazov and their female counterparts Grushenka and Katerina will be virtually neglected for Alexey, the third brother, that less exciting but ever-present figure who sometimes seems to slow up or completely impede the action. Yet I remind you that Alexey is called the hero of the novel, and I suggest that through his character primarily, the author is trying to define new terms for salvation. His character may be got at most easily by describing his relationship with his father.

Alexey's father, Fyodor, would probably be regarded as the most evil of all the characters in the book. He is avaricious and lustful, brooding and lonely, a disagreeable companion in conversation, a great buffoon in society, a notorious, debauched old sinner. He makes a scandalous remark about the church in the presence of clergymen; he has ruthlessly taken the fortune of his first wife; he has neglected, dominated, and abused a second, delicate, slightly unbalanced wife; most shocking of all, he has been said to have raped a helpless idiot girl who later gives birth to Smerdyakov, his ultimate murderer.

Yet, in view of all his crimes, the attitude of his son Alexey is astonishing and unique. Alexey is a mild, gentle, holy youth, who has studied and lived with the monks at the nearby monastery; such a man as his father, one supposes, would baffle and confound and shock him. But the relationship between them is one of love and respect. The father feels "a real and deep affection for him, such as he had never been capable of feeling for anyone before," and says to him, "You're the only creature in the world who has not condemned me." It is Alexey's nature to accept his father on the same terms that Sonia accepts Raskolnikov, without judgment, without censure, with revulsion for the crimes but love for the person.

But this is Alexey's attitude toward and effect on everyone he meets. And the fact that his behavior toward everyone is that of acceptance and understanding, makes him, if I read Dostoevski correctly, a religious figure. Even pain and suffering produce in him the same tolerant response. A young boy to whom he tries to be kind throws stones at him, hitting him once full in the back, and then follows this up by taking a savage bite out of his finger, cutting it to the bone. Though the pain produces a natural cry of anguish and though the boy expects to be attacked and punished for his behavior, Alexey has no thought of revenge but asks simply: "Now tell me, what have I *done* to you?" The absorption in the other person's reasons, the necessity for understanding and sympathizing, fill Alexey always, and

the love people have for him comes partly from his genuine concern for
them and partly from his instinctively honest and sincere responses.

In both these respects, he is the opposite of the underground man,
though I must remind you that both of them are opposite to any kind of
mind in uniform. The mind in uniform of whatever type mistakes itself.
It tries to make romanticism, or social theory, or progress, or scientific
materialism, its rule of life, the basis for its action. But the motivation of
man, Dostoevski says, lies elsewhere, in his will, which drives him to act
counter to all his theories.

The difference between the underground man and the religious man
is this: the motives of the underground man originate in self-concern, in the
necessity for expressing his will, usually in opposition to the particular
mental uniform he is wearing. He has no possibility of securing or helping to secure salvation for anyone but himself. The religious man, on the
other hand, accepting what he finds in others and in himself, expresses his
will in reacting to and helping others, and he can contribute greatly to the
salvation of others.

But these two types are not far apart. It is true that our first thought is
that Alexey and Prince Myshkin in *The Idiot* must be born—elected—not
developed or made; for they seem to be men who by nature are outgoing,
cheerful, full of faith and good will, whereas Raskolnikov and the other
Karamazovs are full of pain and laceration and despair. But a statement by
Father Zossima, the old monk of the nearby monastery, helps to give us
a different slant on these characters:

> There is only one means of salvation; . . . take yourself and make
> yourself responsible for all men's sins, that is the truth, you know,
> friends, for as soon as you sincerely make yourself responsible for
> everything and for all men, you will see at once that it is really so,
> and that you are to blame for every one and for all things. But
> throwing your own indolence and impotence on others you will end
> by sharing the pride of Satan and murmuring against God.

If we look at the plot of *The Brothers*, are we not looking at precisely
this problem? Dmitri and Ivan assume the burden of the murder of their
father, with all the anguish that it entails. Their regeneration depends on
the fact that they *do* assume total and complete responsibility, and underground man and saint join hands in seeking and securing peace of mind.

I cannot bring myself to leave *The Brothers* without referring to Ivan
Karamazov's little parable of the Grand Inquisitor and Christ. Christ returns to the earth and the people recognize him, witness his miracles, follow
him adoring. But the Grand Inquisitor, the most respected religious authority
of his time, seizes him and throws him into prison, without protest from
the populace. He then tells Christ that he must go back where he came from,

that he must not start all the trouble over again. For Christ in resisting the three temptations of the Devil set an impossible model for man. He refused the bread, he refused to throw himself down from the pinnacle of the temple, he refused to covet all the riches of the earth. And his reason for doing so was that he would not bow down, would not *obey* the Devil to receive any of them. And that freedom, says the Grand Inquisitor, is all right for Christ because Christ is God, but for man such terms are too high and must not be permitted. Most people will sell their freedom for bread, some for pride, a few for power. And the only chance of happiness man has, says the Inquisitor, is to make such terms; through obedience, blind obedience, men's lives can be innocent and happy. So Christ is not needed, not wanted, a disturbing force in the world, which can get along only if he is not around. Christ looks at him sorrowfully, silently, as he presents the argument, then goes up and kisses the old man on the lips, and goes away.

This is Ivan's view, not Dostoevski's, and Ivan has much to learn in the course of the novel about himself and freedom of will. But Dostoevski's warning is there all the same. The will of man must express itself; it is the law of life. But salvation can come only if man knows he is expressing his will, only if he does it wilfully and intelligently and honestly no matter how much internal strife and suffering he must undergo. Any attempt to avoid freedom of will and the careful responsibility that goes with it can bring disaster, whether it is made for bread, for ego, for power, or simply because man is tired of fighting.

What I have been saying, it seems to me, is a fairly simple line of argument, though I should warn you that it is in considerable part my own limited view. Why then is Dostoevski often regarded as an enigma? I think the confusion arises in this way: when we read him, our innermost impulses and instincts feel truth in every character, every scene, almost every page. His is the record of our own dark nightmare world of living truth. But his point of view, as I have just been describing it to you, runs counter to all we have persuaded ourselves we believe in. We stand like timorous dwarfs (to borrow a favorite image of the eighteenth century) on the giant shoulders of science and intellect and wonder how in the world we can ever get our feet once more on the ground. And so we look at Dostoevski, instinctively recognize him for the truth-teller that he is, avert our gaze, and pronounce him a mystery.

And yet he will not let us go. He cries to us across eighty years: A world which dares to try to abdicate its personal responsibilities has lost its soul, is beyond danger of damnation or hope of salvation; look to it, he would say, for that way madness—the only expression of the will left to man—that way madness lies.

TOLSTOY

NOVELIST AND MORALIST

EDWARD A. TRAINOR

EARLY ON THE MORNING OF October 29, 1910, Count Leo Tolstoy began the final journey of his life. He set out that day on a last desperate quest for spiritual tranquillity. He was leaving his wife and family and his beloved estate, he told his wife, to "live out my last days in peace and solitude." He wished to emulate the holy men of the East, living simply, spending his days in prayer and contemplation. He was to fail in this, as in so many other things that he attempted. Weak and sick, tortured by the thought that what he was doing was morally wrong, he became seriously ill within days of his departure, and in less than a week, in an upper room of a provincial railroad station, drifted from a morphine-induced sleep into death.

If he had been asked during the last hours of his life to pass judgment upon himself, he would probably have judged himself a failure. The renowned novels he had written, *War and Peace* and *Anna Karenin*, he long before had rejected as meaningless trifles. Once, when he had been lavishly praised as a novelist, he had commented that to praise a man for such work was rather like praising him because he could dance a fine mazurka. More important than his rejection of his artistic achievement was his seeming to call into doubt, during these last days, the moral and ethical dogmas which he had devoted so much of his life to promulgating. The basis of these dogmas was Christian love; yet, as he knew, the final journey was itself motivated by the antithesis of Christian love—selfishness. In order to seek peace, he had caused his wife and family to suffer. To so act, he told one of 'his followers, was to admit moral weakness. All of this must have gone through his mind as he lay dying in that small, stifling room; he may have reflected bitterly that in all he had attempted he had failed.

Paradoxically, if Tolstoy's followers, the men and women who crowded about the railroad station during the last days of Tolstoy's life, had been asked to pass judgment on him, they would have pronounced him a sublime success. To them—indeed to half the world—he was not only the great novelist who had written *War and Peace* and *Anna Karenin*. He was much more. He was the moral teacher who had attempted to change the world, a man so dedicated to the salvation of mankind that at the apex of his career as a novelist he had abandoned novel-writing in order to dedicate his talents to preaching the truth as he saw it. Here was a man who held a position in world literature unequaled in his own time and seldom equaled in history, a man honored and exalted, who had suddenly chucked it all away, rejecting the very novels that had elevated him to this position, to take on the often thankless task of prophet-teacher. Here was a man who, after he had assumed this role, gained not only honor and adulation, but the love and respect of unnumbered multitudes and attention to his pronouncements from world-famous men, such as Bernard Shaw and Henry George, as well as from simple peasants who could neither read nor write. It is little wonder that many of the men and women who kept the death watch would not be able to conceive it possible that Tolstoy was experiencing the anguish of self-doubt.

Our judgment of Leo Tolstoy—the judgment of the majority of people today who are concerned with Tolstoy—is quite different from either his judgment of himself or that pronounced by so many of his contemporaries. On the one hand, we believe that he was one of the world's finest novelists; on the other, we do not accord him the deification conferred upon him by his followers. We are concerned with the artist and lavish abundant praise on him, but tend to forget—or at best minimize—the final phase of Tolstoy's career. Certain works he wrote during this period—"The Kreutzer Sonata," the famous essay on art, *Resurrection*, and any number of short stories—we read and admire; but on the whole we tend to ignore Tolstoy as a moral teacher. We tend to forget that he was not only a man who created two of the most brilliant and penetrating novels in Western literature, but that he was also a man who attempted to create, on earth, a second Eden. The reason for our negligence is obvious: the dogmas he formulated and preached no longer excite the mind. The fundamental errors inherent in them, the errors which Tolstoy toward the end of his life seemed to be dimly aware of, are only too clear to us. Because we for this reason all but dismiss this final phase of Tolstoy's career, we have a less than comprehensive view of Tolstoian thought. In this we do the artist a disservice, and perhaps ourselves also, for the two phases of his career are organically united. The very qualities which made him the novelist we admire are the qualities which forced him to become a moral teacher.

What are the qualities that enable a man to became a great novelist? Basically, a great novelist, it seems to me, must have a quality of mind—of soul if you like—that enables him to see truly and with sympathy into the human situation. He must be able to see man as he really is, neither saint nor sinner, but an intricately wrought synthesis of the two—he must be a person able to understand man's hopes, his lust, his propensity to love and his ability to hate. Coupled with this vision must be a fine sensitivity to the material world in which man moves—the world of shoes and ships and sealing wax, of cabbages and kings. If joined with these twin insights is the ability to recreate this truth through words, then such a person has the potential of a great novelist. Leo Tolstoy was such a person.

That he was endowed with the first of these qualities—the ability to know man truly—is attested by the gallery of Tolstoian characters who are to the readers of his novels as real as the people they associate with every day. Pierre, Natasha, Prince Andrey, the Rostovs, Anna, Count Vronsky—we know, almost intuitively, that each is as men are. We think of them not as characters in a novel but as men and women. Think for a moment of Pierre, the hero of *War and Peace*, if indeed the novel can be said to have a hero. Here is a man as unlike the conventional fictional hero as one can imagine. Given to stoutness, nearsighted, socially gauche, he is not a man to set maidens' hearts fluttering or to fill men's souls with the desire for emulation. Yet maid and man recognize in him themselves. When he foolishly marries the beautiful Princess Ellen, they pity him because they know that man is given to foolish actions; when he embraces enthusiastically the Freemason brotherhood, feeling that in it he has found the peace, the *raison d'etre*, that each man seeks, he reflects their own hopes, their own desires; when he, through the suffering and privation he undergoes as a prisoner with Napoleon's retreating armies, gains wisdom and judgment, he renews in them their faith in their own ability to strive toward maturity. Think for a moment of Anna Karenin, the beautiful, shallow woman who defies her society and her moral code in order to satisfy her desire for Count Vronsky. The reader feels with mounting terror the horror of her situation as he sees her slowly destroyed by the repercussions of her sin. He recognizes that within himself are the same forces which bring about her downfall: he recognizes that man's actions are as often motivated by passion as by reason. Think for a moment of young Rostov during the days before the first battle. He dreams of heroic encounters in which he will play the leading role and from which he will emerge a man, honored and respected. Yet deep within himself he fears, almost to the point of hysterical distraction, that when the moment

of truth comes, when the first call to charge is sounded, he will find that he
is a coward and will run away. So it is with each of them, the wondrous
multitude of characters that Tolstoy created, each painfully human, each
reflecting a knowledge of the stuff of human nature, and each engendering
in the reader, to some degree, an instinctive recognition of the essence of
his own being. This knowledge of man, which his novels so incontestably
demonstrate that Tolstoy possessed, later helped to turn him from the service
of art to the service of God. The doctrine he preached developed, in large
measure, from this knowledge; the impetus to preach it to all mankind
grew out of the love for man that this knowledge inspired.

The second factor which enabled him to be a great novelist, his sensitive
perception of the material world, also played a part in the Tolstoian metamorphosis. That he possessed this sensibility, his works again most brilliantly demonstrate. In the two great novels, *War and Peace* and *Anna
Karenin*, he represents, with the painstaking care of a Persian miniature
painter and the sweep and hugeness of a Rubens, the whole of his world.
Life at the great country houses, the glittering social spectacle of Moscow
and Petersburg, the life of the peasants whose labor made this spectacle
possible, the great military panorama of the Napoleonic wars—almost endless are the vignettes and cycloramas through which he has portrayed his
civilization, each revealing his perception of the life he found around him.
It is difficult in so limited a time to illustrate this particular aspect of his
genius. The best I can hope to do is to suggest something of its essence
through a selection from an early, semi-autobiographical work entitled
Childhood. The narrator of the scene is reflecting on his own childhood, on
a morning when he and his father, who was the owner of a great estate,
set out to hunt and on the way passed through a field in which peasants
were harvesting rye. You will notice in this scene the incisiveness of his
insight into the essence of the situation he is describing, and the sharpness
of his observation of the world about him.

The immeasurable, bright yellow field was closed in only on one side
by a tall, bluish forest which then appeared to me as a most distant
and mysterious place, beyond which either the world came to an end,
or uninhabitable countries began. The whole field was filled with
sheaves and men. Here and there, in the high, thick rye, could be
seen, in a reaped swath, the bent form of a reaping woman. . . ; a
woman in the shade, bending over a cradle; and scattered stacks in the
stubble-field that was overgrown with bluebottles. Elsewhere peasants in nothing but shirts, standing on carts, were loading the sheaves,
and raising the dust on the dry, heated field. The village elder, in
boots and with a camel-hair coat over his shoulders, and notched
sticks in his hand. . . , wiped off his red-haired head and beard with
a towel, and called out loudly to the women. . . . The conversation of

the people, the tramp of the horses, the rattle of the carts, the merry piping of the quails, the buzzing of the insects that hovered in the air in immovable clouds, the odour of wormwood, of straw, and of horses' sweat, thousands of various flowers and of shadows which the burning sun spread over the light-yellow stubble-field, over the blue distance of the forest, and over the light, lilac clouds, the white cobwebs that were borne in the air or that lodged upon the stubbles, —all that I saw, heard, and felt.

This passage does more than simply reveal Tolstoy's brilliance as an observer of the world. It reveals something of his genius as a writer. It suggests how fully he possessed the ability to convey, through words, truth as he apprehended it. Even the translator's pen, as this passage bears witness, cannot destroy the freshness, the vigor and, more important, the rightness of Tolstoy's style. As you read this particular passage, you can almost hear the buzz of the insects and feel the heat of the harvest sun. When you finish reading it, you know something of what one phase of life on the great estates of Russia was like. The passage is not atypical; it is characteristic.

Tolstoy possessed, then, those qualities which I said earlier a great novelist must possess. He had the ability to know, intimately, man and the world in which he lives; he had the ability to present this knowledge in such a way that others could know these things as he knew them. That gift of genius allowed Tolstoy to become one of the Titans of nineteenth-century literature. That gift of genius also led him to shrug off the poet's purple and put on the coarse gown of the moral teacher. It did so because this genius, united with his deeply spiritual nature, forced him to seek the answers to the questions: Why was man created? How is man to live? It forced him to look into his own soul to seek the essence of his own being; it forced him to look at his world, not merely as an observer, but as a searcher after causes and reasons. It set him on a search as horrible and as frightening as Dante's descent into the Inferno.

The world in which he sought reason and pattern was a nightmare world. It was, Tolstoy once stated, divided economically into two classes. There were the rich, indolent, indulgent, extravagant, who took vast wealth from the land without laboring. He wrote: "Everywhere, one or two men in a thousand live in such a way that, without working themselves, they squander and eat up in one day what could feed hundreds of men for a year." On the other hand, there were the poor, the oppressed masses who were too often only a crust of bread away from starvation. Why, he asked himself, should this be so? The answer, he believed, was that in this world it is not the meek who inherit the earth but the strong, the avaricious, the men who can most successfully cheat and steal, the men who are not afraid to use violence and oppression to accomplish their ends.

In the political realm, too, he saw violence and oppression as keystones of national policy, both internal and external. He knew that the prisons of Moscow and Petersburg were filled with men whose crime was that they opposed the State; that the State held the right to take a man's life if he broke its laws; that the ranks of the czarist armies were filled with peasants who had been forcibly inducted; and that wars were waged as a matter of course, men forced to die because the emperor and his generals decreed that the Poles or the Austrians or the Germans were the enemy and must be destroyed.

The church, which in Tolstoy's opinion should have cried out against these evils, not only remained mute but supported and shared in them. The patriarch's palace in Moscow was only a shade less opulent than the czar's; the peasants who worked the great church estates were no less oppressed than those who tilled the fields of the lay landowners; and above all, this institution dedicated to preaching the word of God approved of the murder of human beings, either in war or by State-directed execution. Of this last condition Tolstoy wrote that nothing was so shocking to him as to see that "the representatives of Christ, in their prayers, bless murderers who stand in line, aiming with their rifles at their brothers, and that priests . . . take part in executions and, by their presence, acknowledge the compatibility of manslaughter and Christianity."

To a man so sensitive as Tolstoy such a world was intolerable. He knew man too well and the human situation too intimately not to attempt to reform this world. Publicly he lashed out against these evils and their perpetrators. He wrote, for example, that the "deification of Napoleon, a malefactor, is terrible. Soldiers are animals taught to bite." Of the government he said, "All governments are in equal measure good and evil. The best ideal is anarchy." And in his unfinished work, *The Novel of a Russian Landowner*, he offered a handbook to guide the landowner in the proper treatment of the peasant by brilliantly, almost brutally, delineating the situation as it was and as it should be. The hero of this work abolishes corporal punishment and provides educational opportunities and medical aid for his serfs. He devotes his life not to exploiting them, but to making their lives as happy and as profitable as possible.

Privately, Tolstoy's war against the evils of his world was no less relentless. He made an abortive attempt to institute land reforms on his own estates. He assumed the role of *pater familias* with his peasants, trying to lift from their shoulders the awful burden of their situation, and above all spent much of his time in devising and establishing an educational system which he believed would enable the peasants to free themselves from the economic bondage in which they were held.

More bitter than Tolstoy's struggle to effect reform in the outer world was his struggle to find spiritual peace. He felt a desperate need to find a religious basis for life—an ultimate answer to these questions: Why was man created? To what purpose should he direct his life? This answer he could not find, and terrible was the despair he felt. In a letter written during a period of intense despair he said, "It is strange and awful to say, but I believe in nothing that is taught by religion. And what is more, I not only hate and despise atheism, but I can see no possibility of living, and still less of dying, without faith. As to the exigencies of my brain and the answers of the Christian faith, I find myself in the position of two hands wanting to clasp each other, but the fingers of which resist uniting." Throughout much of his life the hands failed to clasp, plunging the writer into periods of suicidal despair.

Considering this, we might expect *War and Peace* to be a book bitterly reflecting Tolstoy's own frustrated search for a God in whom he could believe. Or, considering the horror with which he beheld the social and political conditions of his world, we might expect it to be an angry novel viciously attacking the evils of society. Surprisingly, it is neither. Although the novel is deeply involved with man's search for the way in which life should be lived, and although it vividly reveals Tolstoy's abhorrence of the evils of society, its concern is far more encompassing than either of these.

The history of the writing of *War and Peace* partially explains why this is so. When he began the novel in 1865, Tolstoy planned to write a rather simple family tale using the Napoleonic wars as a background. As he worked on the book, however, the events of those years when Napoleon swept from Paris to Moscow only to be ignobly defeated and pushed back across the borders of Russia took possession of him. He began to see the possibility of accomplishing a purpose more important than his original one. He became convinced that through this novel he could explain the philosophy of history which he had recently developed and in which he passionately believed.

His view of history is that historical events do not occur because of the will of one man or of a group of men, that they do not occur as a reaction to economic or social events, that in fact all the causes we assign to them are invalid. The flow of history, in his opinion, is predetermined. It follows a pattern which our finite reason cannot discover. Napoleon's invasion of Russia occurred not because he willed it or because it was essential to France's economic position. It occurred simply because it was inevitable—in accordance with some law of nature which we cannot understand.

Once he had determined to demonstrate this thesis in the novel, Tolstoy ceased to think of *War and Peace* as a work in which the life of an aristocratic Russian family during the war era would be examined. He began to think of it as a work in which the life of all Russia, in both peace and war, would be considered. He began to conceive it in epic terms. In full measure he accomplished this later design. Yet at the same time the older conception, that of writing a family novel, was not lost. *War and Peace* recounts the histories of two noble families, the Rostovs and the Bolkonskys, and ends triumphantly in their discovery, after the tribulations of war, of the hope of peace. Their final triumph is in the realization that happiness can be found in living in the country, simply, away from the evils of the court and society. Men who live in this way, Tolstoy states, are living attuned to an indefinable and incomprehensible master plan and will be happy. The reason is, quite simply, that here is the kind of life God intends man to live.

This philosophy is underlined by the histories of the novel's two major heroes, Pierre Bezuhov and Prince Andrey Bolkonsky. Each is actively seeking a way to live a meaningful and happy life. Prince Andrey searches as Tolstoy himself searched, and does not die before he realizes that the peace he is seeking can be found only by returning to the land, man's original habitat, and by living according to his natural instincts, the natural law, which God has instilled in him. Pierre arrives at the same answer, and the narrative closes with him installed at one of his country estates, content in the joys of husbandry and domesticity—living according to the law of nature and of God.

Anna Karenin, the second of the great novels, is like *War and Peace* in its concern with how life should be lived. Levin, Tolstoy's spokesman, seeks to solve the enigma of life as Pierre and Prince Andrey had. His quest, like theirs, ends in the attunement of his life to the natural law as Tolstoy interprets it. Much of the criticism leveled at the structure of the novel loses its validity if it is recognized that *Anna Karenin* is intended to explain this particular view of the good life. The novel is criticized because the two stories told, of Levin's search and of Anna and Count Vronsky, are not organically united. The criticism is meaningless if it is seen that the novelist's intention was to show how living life in opposition to the law of nature leads to despair and tragedy, while living life in accordance with it leads to contentment and happiness.

Tolstoy shows us in *Anna Karenin* how Anna and Count Vronsky, living amid the decadence and falsity of upper-class Russian society, are corrupted by its influence and enter into a morally reprehensible relationship only to find their very love for each other destroyed by jealousy and recrimination. Finally, as a result of their sin, they are themselves destroyed, Anna committing suicide and Vronsky going off to war to seek death. In contrast to these tragic lives, Tolstoy shows us Levin. He, after years of mental turmoil and self-doubt, finds the happiness that eluded Anna and Vronsky by accepting, as Pierre accepts, life as it is meant to be. In devoting himself to his lands and his family, he learns to know happiness, contentment, and peace. It can be seen, I believe, that the two narratives which are found in *Anna Karenin* are necessarily united: the one exemplifying the destiny of man if he does not follow the natural law, and the other his destiny if he does.

A logical question arises at this point: Why or how did Tolstoy arrive at this particular solution to the riddle of life? How was it possible for a man who, as I have pointed out, knew man as few persons have and was deeply sensitive to the evils of the world—how was it possible for him to accept a solution which in effect overcame evil by ignoring it? How could he accept a religious faith that was at best neither universally applicable nor philosophically satisfying? The answer is quite simple. Tolstoy, like the heroes of the novels, found that the solution he proposed in these novels was for him a solution. After his marriage he retired from society to live on one of his estates. There, spending his time in directing the operation of the estate, attempting to alleviate the lot of the peasants, and, above all, enjoying the peace and contentment of domestic life, he found a measure of serenity for his spirit so long tortured by the iniquities of the great world and perplexed by the questionings of his moral nature. It is not surprising that during such a period he could write *War and Peace* and *Anna Karenin*, nor is it surprising that these novels should reflect his faith in the rightness of the particular life he was leading.

Obviously, however, these halcyon days could not long endure. The final chapters of *Anna Karenin*, in fact, seem to signal the end of the idyll. Tolstoy knew in the depths of his heart that beyond the bluish forest that bounded his brilliantly yellow fields was not a "distant mysterious place beyond which either the world came to an end or uninhabited countries began." Beyond were all the horror and ugliness that had so long weighed upon him. Not for long could this man be content to stand apart, doing nothing to combat the forces which were in his opinion destroying man. Above all, not for long could he quiet his troubled spirit with a religious faith so negative, so lacking in substance.

It is not surprising then that this golden interlude lasted for only a few years, that soon the shadows again shut out the sun. Nor is it surprising that the shadows were darker, the burdens weighing upon his soul greater. He was like a man entering a darkened house from a brilliantly sunlit street. Never is the contrast between the two so great as at that moment. So it was when Tolstoy re-entered the house of spiritual darkness. He was, at the time, so overcome with this "moral disease," as he termed it, that he contemplated taking his own life. All the terrifying questions that had in the past caused him so much misery flooded back into his mind. Why is humanity divided "into two classes, one working, oppressed, living in misery and suffering, and a second which is idle, oppressing, living in abundance?" Why do "the

wicked always have power over the good, or at least the less wicked?" Why
are men so thoughtless that they believe that the titles of prince, of minister,
of governor are something real and very important? Why are "men who call
themselves Christians and who thus profess liberty, equality, and fraternity
prepared . . . to kill their brothers?" Why does the church, with a cross,
which symbolizes the cross on which Christ died, bless the evil rampant in
the world—the evil symbolized by the soldier, the landowner, the ruler? And
finally the most important question recurred: Why was man created? To
what purpose should he direct his life?

Out of the misery of these dark days, out of the bitterness of this self-
interrogation, Tolstoy emerged with an answer, a solution to the enigmas of
life. In the teachings of Christianity he found the reasons for man's creation;
there too was revealed how life should be lived, to what purpose it should be
directed. The world was as it was, he became convinced, only because man
did not follow the basic, primary command of Christ: *love one another*. Paul
Roubiczek, to whose book *The Misinterpretation of Man* I am indebted for
calling to my attention many of the Tolstoian social, political, and moral pronouncements quoted in this lecture and for its brilliant discussion of these
pronouncements, as well as the entire Tolstoian metamorphosis, sums up
Tolstoy's convictions in these words: "If the most important command . . .
were generally obeyed, it would be enough in itself to free and redeem mankind. The most perfect social utopias would be easy to accomplish if men
were willing to help one another and if they were guided by a living sense
of community, strong enough to overcome their selfishness." Once he had
arrived at this conviction, his mission, as he saw it, was not only to promul-
gate this doctrine but to convince mankind that general adherence to it is not
an unobtainable goal; that every man has the strength to strive toward this
goal; that because he has the strength, he has the duty. The life of man must
be recast; each man must rebuild his life, basing his new life on his acceptance of this command of Christ. Tolstoy felt—with the fervor of an Old
Testament prophet—that the world must recognize this. "For," he stated,
"not before every single man makes the Christian way of life his own and
begins to live accordingly, will the contradictions of human life be solved
and a new way of human life created."

As a corollary to this basic dogma—love one another—Tolstoy postulated
another, again using the words of Christ to express it. The second tenet of
his creed is: *resist not evil*. By this he meant that one should not fight against
the evils rampant in the world, should not attempt by revolt or indeed any
overt act to change the world. Seek, Tolstoy told his followers, only to change
yourselves. Seek to root from your hearts all that is contrary to Christian love.
Dissociate yourselves from all that is evil, refuse to serve the State, refuse to
profit by another's labor, refuse to attend a church that distorts the word of

God, but do not take up arms against any of these. As Tolstoy became more deeply involved with these doctrines, the philosophy he preached took on the appearance of a new religion. The bible of the religion was the Christian Bible, but its god was not Jesus Christ, whom Tolstoy stripped of his divinity, but an almost completely depersonalized principle of Good. The rule of life he laid down for the faithful was very similar to Christian monasticism, stressing poverty, manual labor, moral self-perfection, and celibacy. It differed from Christian monasticism in that it condemned any activity that did not directly contribute to the moral growth of the individual. The painter, the poet, the composer, the inventor must, according to the dogma of the Tolstoian Christianity, abandon his art, for it does not help to make him a more perfect moral being.

It is difficult to comprehend with what fanatic zeal Tolstoy set about the task of giving to mankind these truths which he had culled from his spiritual searching. The quality of mind that enabled him to see truly and with sympathy into the human situation—the quality of soul which set him off on his spiritual quest, the quality that enabled him to be a great writer—this quality now acted as a spur, goading him on. Mankind must be saved, and it could be saved only if it could be made to see that Christian love, with all its moral implications, was the means to salvation.

The tremendous energies that he had once devoted to his novels were now devoted to this greater task. Didactic writing after didactic writing flowed from his pen, each dedicated to making clear to man the rightness and the necessity of Tolstoian Christianity. He no longer had the time, and soon not even the inclination, to write novels. There were too many essential things to do. The tragedy of this situation is manifold. A talent which had the ability to reveal so clearly and brilliantly the heart of man was to an appreciable extent put to another use. The religion that it served, the faith in which Tolstoy had such faith, scarcely outlived his death. Although it had some effect on later thinkers, notable among them Gandhi, the Indian philosopher-teacher, it caused, in the long run, scarcely a ripple in the tide of Western thought. Tragedy of tragedies, this faith did not even give to Tolstoy himself the peace of soul he had so long sought. While he preached poverty, he lived, because he could not bear to hurt his wife and family, among the outer trappings of vast wealth; while he preached that the only labor morally profitable to man was manual labor, he continued, to some degree deliberately, to serve through his writings his artistic conscience as well as his moral purpose; and while he preached Christian love, during the last days of his life he sinned against this commandment by leaving his wife and family, knowing full well the pain his action would cause. As he so brilliantly reveals in *The Light That Shines in Darkness*, he found in his role of prophet-teacher not profound peace but gnawing frustration.

The reason that this was true, although Tolstoy never realized it, is that the religion he preached is a religion for angels, not men. It is based on a penetrating understanding of the moral nature of man but on a totally obtuse view of his physical and aesthetic natures. Because it condemns man to develop only his spiritual potential, it was doomed to failure from its inception. It is the supreme paradox that a spiritual quest that grew out of a wondrous ability to see clearly man and the human situation should end in a religion that denied man's humanity. That this happened is the tragedy of Leo Tolstoy.

Yet Leo Tolstoy was in no sense a failure. The two great novels he wrote, *War and Peace* and *Anna Karenin*, stand today, rightfully, among the great works of Western civilization. They are great because they illuminate with brilliance and sensitivity the mind and soul of Western man. Leo Tolstoy today is rightly considered one of the great men of Western civilization. His greatness is not only in the novels he created; it is as well in the life that he lived. This life, characterized by a tireless and painful search after truth, epitomizes the spirit which has given Western civilization its form and direction.

If, during the last hours of his life, Tolstoy pronounced himself a failure, a man defeated, he would have found consolation if he had remembered a sentence from Montaigne, a philosopher he deeply admired. "There are defeats," Montaigne wrote, "more triumphant than victories." If Tolstoy died defeated, such certainly was the defeat.

SOME CHARACTERISTICS
OF HARDY'S NOVELS

ROBERT C. SLACK

THE LAST HALF OF THE NINETEENTH CENTURY and the first quarter of
the twentieth form a transition era, the era in which the modern world
came into being. The lifetime of Thomas Hardy covers the entire span, and
more. He was born in 1840 (the young Queen Victoria had been crowned
only three years before); and he lived to the considerable age of eighty-
seven, until 1928. When Hardy was a youth there were no automobiles; the
railway system in England was just beginning; there were no airplanes;
there were no public telegraphs, no telephones, no radios. Women did not
have the right to vote; indeed, they had few rights at all. No Einstein had
arisen to upset man's conceptions of the physical world; no Darwin, to upset his conceptions of the spiritual world; no Freud, to upset his conceptions
of the world within his mind. Within Hardy's lifetime all these changes
came about, and they were accompanied by radical shifts in man's way of
regarding his universe and his place in it. Before Hardy's death, T. S. Eliot
had written "The Waste Land," Hemingway had written *The Sun Also
Rises*, Irving Berlin had written "All Alone by the Telephone." We were in
the modern world.

Hardy's novels reflect this vast change. Though not all of them bear
clearly the imprint of the future, there is an erratic but perceivable development until he ends his novel-writing in 1895 with what may be defended as
a virtually "modern" work, *Jude the Obscure*. Hardy did push the novel
along in the ways it was to go; also, he reflected the climate of advanced

opinion of his own time; yet in tradition and spirit his work shows an almost direct inheritance from Elizabethan drama. Any one of these strands—the past, the present, or the future as reflected in Hardy's novels—bears exploration. But to study any one without considering the other two would be false. It would be no fair picture of Hardy's accomplishment to paint him simply as a forerunner of the moderns, for instance. So I shall try here to look at his novels as they carry on traditions of the past, as they reflect his present, and as they anticipate the future (what we call the modern world).

If you begin reading almost any Hardy novel now—say, *The Return of the Native* or *Far from the Madding Crowd*—it will not be long before you are struck by a certain archaic quality, something that is not Now, not modern, not Twentieth Century. You will probably find it first in the plot. Hardy's novels *have* plots, in the old-fashioned sense. By old-fashioned, I do not mean the fashion of Hardy's day; by then George Eliot had shown the way to a new realistic tradition. No, Hardy was old-fashioned in his own day. Lord David Cecil in *Hardy the Novelist* has shown that Hardy reached back to a conception of the novel which, like Fielding's, was closely related to the tradition of drama—a tradition marked usually by a nonrealistic plot, consisting of intrigue and sensational events all resolved neatly in the last pages, and often by a cast of comic characters who offer relief from the serious tensions of the story. In addition to adopting a concept of story derived from Elizabethan drama (with more than a few elements of classical Greek tragedy thrown in), Hardy, like Walter Scott, loved such ancient folk tales as were memorialized in old ballads, full of despairing lovers, betrayed maidens, drownings, superstition, and witchcraft.

One other strand, central and prominent in all his work, must be woven into Hardy's derivations from the past: the pastoral tradition. Certainly no novelist has portrayed more faithfully or lovingly the natural beauty of the English countryside in which the middle-class rural yeoman has his roots and being.

Put the pastoral scene, the old dramatic-plot tradition, and the devices of folk tradition together, throw in a dash of classical tragedy, and you get something that approximates Hardy's form of the novel. As an example, consider *The Return of the Native*. Egdon Heath, somber and timeless, broods over the whole story. The plot is clearly dramatic, culminating in a tragic catharsis. Eustacia Vye—beautiful, queenly, passionate Eustacia—who hates Egdon Heath, falls in love with and marries Clym Yeobright, who loves the heath and its people so much that he has returned from Paris to devote his life to teaching his neighbors in a small school he is going to open there. Eustacia knows what plans Clym has, but she believes she can coax him away from them after they are married. Symbolically, they become engaged during an eclipse of the moon.

A marriage between so divergent a couple has very little chance of succeeding, at best. And then, through a series of remarkable coincidences, Eustacia unwittingly causes the death of her husband's mother. Clym harrows her with accusations, and she leaves him to return to her grandfather's home. Clym is sorry and writes her a letter seeking reconciliation. But Eustacia, through coincidence again, misses seeing his letter and undertakes to run away with her former lover. A driving rain is beating down. As she pushes on through the night to meet her former lover she cries out in misery: " 'How I have tried and tried to be a splendid woman, and how destiny has been against me! . . .I do not deserve my lot! . . .O, the cruelty of putting me into this ill-conceived world! I was capable of much; but I have been injured and blighted and crushed by things beyond my control! O, how hard it is of Heaven to devise such tortures for me, who have done no harm to Heaven at all!' " Here the novel form has been raised as close as it ever has been to the glorious eloquence of a soul in torment which we find in Greek tragedy. Eustacia drowns in a rain-swollen weir, and her lover with her; Yeobright, who has tried to rescue them, barely survives. Yeobright lives on, a saddened man who chooses to become an itinerant preacher.

From this brief résumé, it is apparent that the plot is highly dramatic, rising to a poetic grandeur akin to that of Elizabethan or Greek tragedy. Far from being low-toned realism, the story is really an unusual sequence of events, striking in their own nature. Hardy knew what he was doing. In some notes on fiction writing he says: "The recent school of novel-writers . . . forget in their insistence on life, and nothing but life, in a plain slice, that a story *must be worth the telling*, that a good deal of life is not worth any such thing. . . ." "We tale-tellers are all Ancient Mariners, and none of us is warranted in stopping Wedding Guests (in other words, the hurrying public) unless he has something more unusual to relate than the ordinary experience of every average man and woman."

A great deal of the charm and the magic poetic power of Hardy's books comes from an emphasis on the unusual. In *The Return of the Native*, Hardy gives us the solid, helping-hand character Diggory Venn in a strange, unforgettable guise. Diggory Venn is essentially a good, true-hearted young man who has become a reddleman, a journeyman seller of red ochre powder. He travels about the countryside alone in his red-stained van—he himself dyed a brilliant red from head to toe. The children of the heath think the reddleman is the devil himself; and when Venn appears suddenly in the firelight one night he gives fright to a good many of the adults, too. Throughout the book, Diggory Venn is a mysterious character, appearing unexpectedly to do a good turn and then vanishing back into the mystery of the heath.

The poetic aura of the book is enhanced too by Hardy's use of folk custom and superstition. The Christmas mummers' play of St. George and the Turkish Knight given at the Yeobrights' party goes back in English folk history to the Middle Ages; indeed, the practice of mumming is said to be derived from the Romans. The folk custom of lighting bonfires on the night of November 5 (Guy Fawkes day) is linked by Hardy with funeral pyres of the antique Britons and the festival fires lighted ages ago for Thor and Woden. Folk superstitions are given a personal directness when Susan Nunsuch stabs Eustacia with a long stocking-needle because she believes Eustacia is a witch who has been charming her child. Later, on the stormy night on which Eustacia tries to run away, we see Susan putting a curse on her by sticking pins in a little wax image and then melting it over the fire as she intones the Lord's Prayer backwards. When Eustacia meets her death only minutes later, we remember Susan's wax image with a little shudder.

Another element in the tradition of poetic tragedy, especially that of Shakespeare, is the use of comic relief. We remember the drunken porter in *Macbeth* just after the harrowing murder of the king. A knocking at the gate drags out the poor alcoholic dishrag of a porter, who staggers around dazed but amazingly voluble; and this burlesque comic temporarily relieves the tension for the audience. And we remember that Hamlet's gravediggers appear after the pathetic madness and drowning of Ophelia. Hardy's tragedy has its comics, too. They are not always used to relieve the intensity of immediate tragic moments—but they are clearly lineal descendants of Shakespeare's crew. There is Grandfer Cantle, a "mouldy weasand of such a old man," as one of his companions calls him, boasting of what a pretty sight of a soldier he had been back "in the year four." And there is his thin-blooded offspring, Christian Cantle, the fearful, twisted, half-idiot freak, afraid of his own shadow, loved by no woman, with his big bulging eyes and his mop of unruly hair. He was "thirty-one last tatie-digging." At least, he says,

> "That's my age by baptism, because that's put down in the great book of the Judgment that they keep in church vestry; but mother told me I was born some time afore I was christened."
> "Ah!"
> "But she couldn't tell when, to save her life, except that there was no moon . . . . Mother know'd 'twas no moon, for she asked another woman that had an almanac, as she did whenever a boy was born to her, because of the saying, 'No moon, no man' . . . . I'd sooner go without drink at Lammas-tide than be a man of no moon."

Hardy's rustic characters, though generally comic, are akin to the chorus in classical Greek tragedy. They give us a generous amount of humor for a while, but they almost always get around to talking about the main characters and giving us information or speculation about them.

The Return of the Native is one of the most characteristic of Hardy's novels. And it shows clearly that Hardy's art, in form and aesthetic effect, is closely tied to old traditions—the pastoral, Elizabethan and Greek tragedy, and folk tales and customs. To say that the traditions are old ones is no disparagement. They are the source of a great deal of his charm and power.

But though he adopted a form and a blend of artistic traditions tied closely to the past, Hardy, in content, was very much in the current of advanced opinion of his day. He was twenty before this current caught him up; indeed, there wasn't much in his early environment to make a rebel of him. The Oxford Movement of 1833-45 had succeeded in revitalizing religious feelings, and the years from 1840 to 1860 saw in England a remarkable revival of religious faith. Men were confident of the God they believed in. Hardy's home, the shire of Dorset, was not unaware of the great movement. The *Dorset County Chronicle* followed the theological awakening with acute interest; Harvey Curtis Webster in *On a Darkling Plain* gives a characteristic statement of a contributor: "The history of the Church is the fulfillment of God's will for the salvation of man, the accomplishment of prophecies, the triumph of grace over the imperfections and sins of nature." This statement might be considered a fairly accurate summary of Hardy's own beliefs up to the age of twenty. He regularly attended the Stinsford Church, in which the influence of the Oxford Movement was strong; he taught Sunday school, and for some years looked forward to entering the ministry. As a youth he seems to have had a fairly optimistic outlook. He read by choice the romancers, Ainsworth, G. P. R. James, and Dumas *père*—who all held the view that life was a kind of Paradise. For them poetic justice always prevailed. As Webster puts it, "The good [people] . . . prosper and marry the inconceivably lovely, faithful, and virtuous heroines; the bad always deserve their unhappy fate."

Hardy, then, was a young man remarkably ripe for disillusionment. And the disillusionment came. It began chiefly because of two books which appeared within the space of a single year, the year that Hardy became twenty. Both were introduced to him by his young friend Horace Moule, recently graduated from Cambridge. One was the famous *Essays and Reviews* by "The Seven against Christ," as the authors came to be nicknamed. The *Essays* were denounced as atheistic and were the center of rabid controversy from the time of their appearance in 1860. The other was Charles Darwin's *Origin of Species*. In that book Hardy found the theory that "animals are descended from at most only four or five progenitors and plants from an equal or lesser number," and that variations in the living kingdom first arose as accidental freaks. He found a portrayal of the struggle for existence as the essential condition of nature. Darwin believed that in this cruel struggle only the fittest survived, the fittest being the strongest, or fiercest, or most cunning.

So in a single impressionable year Hardy encountered the strongest expression of rationalistic doubts concerning revealed religion that the century had yet produced, and the powerful theories of Darwin, which suggested that man, rather than being the deliberate product of a beneficent Creator, was really a survivor of a long accidental process governed more by chance than plan; that nature, rather than being a kindly mother, really operated by the law of mutual butchery. These books affected Hardy mightily. Later he was to read the agnostic writings of John Stuart Mill and Herbert Spencer, and the ironical historian Gibbon. But the chief impetus behind Hardy's disenchantment with the universe probably came from Darwin and the *Essays and Reviews*.

Out of his intellectual disillusionment, and nourished by his natural inclination toward the pessimistic, a dark view of the universe grew within his mind. This is the universe he paints in his novels. Man, far from being in Somebody's kindly hand, finds himself in an indifferent universe, where he must expect to find happiness only an occasional episode in a general drama of pain. Sometimes Hardy suggests that the universe is not merely indifferent but downright mean, as in the ending of the tragic story of poor Tess Durbeyfield. " 'Justice' was done," writes Hardy, "and the President of the Immortals . . . had ended his sport with Tess." And Fate plays nasty tricks on Michael Henchard, the mayor of Casterbridge. It is only on the morning after Henchard discovers that Elizabeth-Jane is *not* truly his daughter that she comes to him and accepts him as her father. "The moment and the act he had contemplated for weeks with a thrill of pleasure . . . and the fruition of the whole scheme was such dust and ashes as this."

Hardy's frequent employment of coincidence is deliberate. He sees Fate acting through coincidence; but Chance, meaningless Chance, often seems to dole out the bread to one house and the children to another. So in the novels, Chance seems to operate often with an ironic purpose. In *Desperate Remedies* Aeneas Manston misreads a railroad timetable and as a result fails to meet his wife's train, starting a chain of accidental circumstances which lead to her death. In *Tess of the d'Urbervilles*, Tess slips under her lover's door a letter which would avert her tragedy; but the carpet's edge reaches to the door and the letter slips under the carpet too, never to be seen. Pure chance—yet, like the chance freaks in Darwin's theory which lead to the formation of a new species, these happenings attain a tremendous significance in the light of later knowledge.

Hardy could admit man as an accidental figment of creation in an indifferent universe—but he believed it an intolerable cruelty that nature should have given this figment feelings: feelings which could be rubbed raw by the injustices and brutalities of human existence. Poor Tess Durbeyfield learned too late that men are deceivers ever. If only she had listened to certain wise texts, which she (like the world in general) certainly had heard, she would not have been imposed on. "But it had not been in Tess's power —nor is it in anybody's power—to feel the whole truth of golden opinions while it is possible to profit by them. She—and how many more—might have ironically said to God with Saint Augustine: 'Thou hast counselled a better course than Thou hast permitted.' " Tess's mother, in her stoic peasant way, recognizes that this *is* the way life operates. After Tess's downfall, she says only, "Well, we must make the best of it, I suppose. 'Tis nater, after all, and what do please God!"

But the scheme of things didn't please Thomas Hardy. "Nature does not often say 'See!' to her poor creature at a time when seeing can lead to happy doing; or reply 'Here!' to a body's cry of 'Where?' till the hide-and-seek has become an irksome, outgrown game." This is darkly pessimistic, no doubt. But in fairness one aspect of Hardy's pessimism should be underlined: he is *not* cynical about mankind; he is no embittered misanthrope. There are only one or two really unsympathetic people, real scoundrels, in the whole body of Hardy's novels; whereas there are a whole host of admirable, strong, true-hearted men and of lovely, sensitive women. For Gabriel Oak, Clym Yeobright, Michael Henchard, Jude Fawley, Bathsheba Everdene, Tess Durbeyfield, Sue Bridehead; for practically all of his men and women; for *all* the animal world so kindly seen in everything he wrote, even for the trees and the grass and the flowers—for every living thing Hardy shows intense respect and a deep love.

So Hardy's pessimism does not arise out of a personal hatred of life, but out of the much nobler emotion of pity. And also out of a desire to better conditions if the way can be found. In one of his poems he has written, ". . . if a way to the Better there be, it exacts a full look at the Worst." Plainly he thought of himself not as a pessimist, but as a meliorist —one who seeks a way to mend this sorry scheme of things.

What I have said so far pertains to all the novels of Thomas Hardy except the last, *Jude the Obscure. Jude*, by virtue of some strange virus in its veins, is a "modern" novel—published in 1895 though it was—and it is the only one of the whole Hardy canon of which this might be said. *Jude* is not Hardy's best novel. *The Return of the Native* and *Far from the Madding Crowd* are more likely candidates for that title; and I personally have found *Tess of the d'Urbervilles* the most powerfully moving of his works. But *Jude* still is a great book, and it has here-and-nowness that is not quite felt in the others.

What makes a novel "modern" in temper? This is too broad a question to be answered fully here, but there are two qualities that we have learned to expect: a frank, realistic treatment of sex and a sharp social consciousness. *Jude* has both. And it was a stunner for 1895. Jeannette Gilder, "a maiden

lady" writing for the *New York World*, cried out: "What has happened to
Thomas Hardy? . . . I thought that *Tess of the d'Urbervilles* was bad
enough, but that is milk for babes compared to this. . . . Aside from its immorality there is coarseness which is beyond belief. . . . When I finished the
story I opened the windows and let in the fresh air, and I turned to my
bookshelves and I said: 'Thank God for Kipling and Stevenson, Barrie and
Mrs. Humphry Ward. Here are four great writers who have never trailed
their talents in the dirt.' "

The Bishop of Wakefield said he had burned the book.

But some voices of support arose in the storm. Swinburne wrote to
Hardy, "The tragedy . . . is equally beautiful and terrible in its pathos."
Havelock Ellis published a defense of the novel. The fact that the English
people wanted to apply a set of barnyard morals to their own love lives
was not Mr. Hardy's fault, said Mr. Ellis; and when Hardy broached an en-
lightened view of the problem, they were worse than foolish to be offended.
It is doubtful that Ellis soothed any of the ruffled feelings of 1895. The main
outcry was at first certainly against the book; and this, plus the reaction to
Tess of the d'Urbervilles, had a great deal to do with Hardy's never writing
another novel. "A man must be a fool," he said, "to deliberately stand up
to be shot at." Besides, he had always wanted to write poetry. So he turned
to that.

Jude is the story of a young man who dreamed of going to Oxford. The
university is called Christminster in the novel, but it is Oxford all the same.
He is a poor boy brought up by an aunt who keeps a small bakery shop.
Jude studies as he drives the bakery cart. Fired by an ideal of scholarship,
he painfully teaches himself Latin and Greek from old, out-of-date text-
books he has managed to pick up.

When he becomes nineteen, he believes he is about prepared to set
off for Christminster. At that point in his life he is spied by a buxom
country maiden named Arabella Donn, "a complete and substantial female
animal." They meet, their eyes cross, and she resolves to have him: "He's
the sort of man I long for. I shall go mad if I can't give myself to him altogether!" she cries. Her friends, who seem to have acquired more knowledge
of the world than Arabella has, whisper significant things into her ear; and
a few months later poor Jude finds himself forced to marry this unsuitable
mate—selling his books to buy saucepans.

"And so . . . ," writes Hardy, "the two swore that at every other time of
their lives till death took them, they would assuredly believe, feel, and desire precisely as they had believed, felt, and desired during the few preceding
weeks. What was as remarkable as the undertaking itself was the fact that
nobody seemed at all surprised at what they swore." When Jude discovers
a few weeks later that Arabella is *not* going to have a child, that she was,

as she says, "mistaken" about the matter, he realizes that he has been caught in a trap—partly by an instinct in him which (he thinks) "had nothing in it of the nature of vice," and partly by the customs of society. Not long after, Arabella tires of Jude, quarrels with him, and leaves him, emigrating to Australia with her father.

Jude tries to gather up the strands of his life—after one period of severe depression in which he attempts suicide. And at last he sets off for Christminster. There he finds himself in for bitter disillusionment. He has been told that such places are "only for them with plenty o' money," but he will not believe it. He selects five university dons whom he has seen about the city and who look to him like kindly men, and he writes five letters, asking their advice. There is a long wait, and at last only one reply. The reply is merely: "Sir— . . . judging from your description of yourself as a working-man, I venture to think that you will have a much better chance of success in life by remaining in your own sphere and sticking to your trade than by adopting any other course. . . ."

Jude is crushed. He rushes out to a tavern and attempts to find relief in drink. This does not help, however, and he ends the bitter night by scrawling, with a piece of chalk, on the college walls: " 'I have understanding as well as you, I am not inferior to you: yea, who knoweth not such things as these?'—Job xii. 3." So his hopes of scholarship are smothered.

In Christminster he meets his cousin, Sue Bridehead, and instantly he is in love with her. That love is the next and the final determining drive in the character of Jude. She is attracted to him; but eventually he has to tell her he has a wife. This drives Sue into an ill-advised marriage with the schoolmaster Phillotson, a man much older than she. She finds her husband repulsive and begs him to release her so that she can go to her cousin Jude. Phillotson is shocked by this unheard-of attitude; but after she jumps out the window one night when he has absentmindedly stepped into her room he sorrowfully but broadmindedly consents to her leaving.

Sue goes to Jude, and the two of them have the strangest kind of companionship. Jude naturally expects that they will be lovers in a physical sense, but much to his surprise and annoyance Sue demurs. "O Jude!" she says, "I didn't mean that! . . . don't press me and criticize me, Jude! Assume that I haven't the courage of my opinions . . . it is a delight in being with you, of a supremely delicate kind, and I don't want to go further and risk it by—an attempt to intensify it! . . . Don't discuss it further, dear Jude!" However, eventually Jude does have his way. Later they both become divorced from their mates. But by this time they both have developed a fear of marriage, and they never can bring themselves to the actual contract. They try—but when they go to the registrar's office they see a pair that had arrived earlier to be married: a sullen soldier with a sad and timid bride;

she was soon obviously to become a mother, and she had a black eye. Then they see another couple there: a jailbird, just out this morning, marrying the woman who met him at the jail gates and brought him straight there; she is paying for everything. They are horrified by the sordid business and cannot go through with it. They believe that in fifty, even in twenty years, people will begin to feel as they do about the social contract of marriage.

So Sue and Jude never do manage to marry.

Then suddenly Jude learns that after Arabella had left him, she had borne him a son; and on the heels of the information, Arabella's son appears. The boy is a symbol and one of Hardy's most poorly realized characters. Morbid, brooding, seeing only the worst, he is called Little Father Time. He looks at a playful kitten at which everyone is laughing—but his sad eyes seem to say only, "All laughing comes from misapprehension. Rightly looked at there is no laughable thing under the sun." Sue and Jude take the boy to the Agricultural Show, but he is not cheered. "I am very, very sorry. . . ," he says. "But please don't mind!—I can't help it. I should like the flowers very much, if I didn't keep on thinking they'd be all withered in a few days!"

As the years go on, Sue and Jude have two children of their own; but their unconventional relationship and Sue's thoughtless honesty, which insists that she sooner or later tell people they are not married, forces them to move from one city to another. The supreme tragic horror comes when Sue thoughtlessly tells Father Time that another child is on the way. The morbid boy decides that he and the other two children are the cause of all the family troubles, and he hangs the other two and himself. At the very moment the dead children are discovered Jude can hear, through the wall of the house, the chapel organist practicing next door. "It's the anthem from the seventy-third Psalm," he says; " 'Truly God is loving unto Israel.' " (Early readers thought this horrible scene grotesque and impossible. Yet Hardy's American friend Rebecca Owen pasted a newspaper clipping in her copy of *Jude* telling of just such a murder and suicide by a boy in France, only a year after *Jude* was published.)

This tragedy breaks Sue. From being a free-thinker—as Jude calls her, "a woman-poet, a woman-seer, a woman whose soul shone like a diamond"— she comes to conceive of herself as a vile sinner, turns to a narrow and dogmatic religious frenzy and breaks away from Jude. In self-flagellation she returns to the old schoolmaster Phillotson, who still loves her, and marries him once more.

Jude takes to drink, and, to complete the irony, Arabella comes upon him while he is out of his wits and contrives to have him remarry her. Not long after, Jude sickens and dies at the age of twenty-nine. His last words are the bitter lamentation from *Job*: "Let the day perish wherein I was born,

and the night in which it was said, There is a man child conceived. . . .
Wherefore is light given to him that is in misery, and life unto the bitter
in soul?"

The novel is tragic, but not with archaic overtones. *Jude* is a book with a
sense of immediacy about it. Gone is the pastoral tradition: the characteristic
setting is urban. Gone are the amusing rustics. And consider the problems
the book does deal with. In his *Thomas Hardy* Albert Guerard has made a
convenient listing of them. There is the social and economic problem of
educational opportunities for the poor. Jude (he is only a poor laborer)
never has a chance to get the higher learning of which he dreams. There
is the problem of marriage and divorce. Both Jude and Sue feel trapped by
the contract of marriage, and they feel that a purer bond based upon active
and living love is the only bond that sensitive and intelligent human beings
should honor. There are psychological problems aplenty. Jude's sexuality
and his urge to self-destruction obsess him throughout the book. Sue, on the
other hand, is a strange nature weakly sexed but possessed by a compulsive
desire to attract men. "Sometimes," she confesses to Jude, "a woman's *love
of being loved* gets the better of her conscience, and though she is agonized
at the thought of treating a man cruelly, she encourages him to love her while
she doesn't love him at all." Hardy calls Sue "an epicure in emotions," and
Sue speaks of "my curiosity to hunt up a new sensation." Writing about
Sue later in a letter, Hardy says: "There is nothing perverted or depraved
in Sue's nature. The abnormalism consists in disproportion, not in inversion,
her sexual instinct being healthy as far as it goes, but unusually weak and
fastidious. Her sensibilities remain painfully alert notwithstanding, as they
do in nature with such women." There are also religious problems, ethical
problems, and the spiritual problems—peculiarly modern—of unrest, intro-
spectiveness, melancholy, and isolation.

From this brief summary of the problems with which *Jude* concerns itself, it should be amply clear why this novel was far ahead of its time in
1895. What Hardy might have progressed to next, had he continued to
write novels, is difficult to say. He turned to poetry at the age of fifty-six
and became one of the significant poets of the twentieth century. But that
is another story.

At the age of seventy-five, he published a little poem called "The Oxen."

> Christmas Eve, and twelve of the clock.
>   "Now they are all on their knees,"
> An elder said as we sat in a flock
>   By the embers in hearthside ease.
>
> We pictured the meek mild creatures where
>   They dwelt in their strawy pen,

Nor did it occur to one of us there
　To doubt they were kneeling then.

So fair a fancy few would weave
　In these years! Yet I feel,
If someone said on Christmas Eve,
　"Come; see the oxen kneel,

"In the lonely barton by yonder coomb
　Our childhood used to know,"
I should go with him in the gloom,
　Hoping it might be so.

Even so late in his life Hardy still hoped that it might be so. He would have *liked* to have the faith of the little child; it is important to remember that he cared so deeply about the simple faiths of his childhood. And every time the cold white light of his intellect looked about him and determined that his childhood faith could not be justified by the experience of mankind, it was a painful personal wound.

This we should remember: behind the iconoclast who tore the veil from the temple and shocked his generation—behind the congenital pessimist who howled in the Cave of Despair—stood a sorrowful, tender-hearted little man, the man who took as his epigraph for the tragic story of Tess,

" 'Poor wounded name! My bosom as a bed
Shall lodge thee.' "

THEODORE DREISER
AND THE AMERICAN DREAM

DONALD M. GOODFELLOW

WHEN THEODORE DREISER, then twenty-two, arrived in Pittsburgh, he hoped to find nothing more than a job as a reporter on one of the newspapers. A quarter of a century later he wrote: "Of all the cities in which I ever worked or lived, Pittsburgh was the most agreeable. Perhaps it was due to the fact that my stay included only spring, summer, and fall, or that I found a peculiarly easy newspaper atmosphere, or that the city was so different physically from any I had thus far seen; but . . . certainly no other newspaper work I ever did seemed so pleasant, no other city more interesting."

Undoubtedly Dreiser's pleasant recollections were due in part to the opportunity to attempt something for the Pittsburgh *Dispatch* more literary than he had been permitted to do for Chicago and St. Louis papers—"a series of mood or word pictures about the most trivial matters—a summer storm, a spring day, a visit to a hospital, the death of an old switchman's dog, the arrival of the first mosquito." These little sketches gave him his "first taste of what it means to be a creative writer." And one afternoon, having nothing else to do, he wandered into the Allegheny Carnegie Library and by the merest chance picked up one of Balzac's novels. As he began reading, "a new and inviting door to life" was suddenly thrown open to him. "Not only for the brilliant and incisive manner with which Balzac grasped life and invented themes whereby to present it, but for the fact that the types he handled with most enthusiasm and skill—the brooding, seeking, ambitious beginner in life's social, political, artistic and commercial affairs— were, I thought, so much like myself." In that characterization of Balzac's

types are summarized the types that Dreiser was to portray in his novels—
types that were so much like himself, no matter from what walks of life they
came or what heights or depths they attained.

Equally important in directing Dreiser's thoughts during his Pittsburgh
days were the writings of Huxley, Tyndall, and Spencer, which he also discovered in the library. "Up to this time," he wrote,

> there had been in me a blazing and unchecked desire to get on and
> the feeling that in doing so we did get somewhere; now in its place
> was the definite conviction that spiritually one got nowhere, that
> there was no hereafter, that one lived and had his being because
> one had to, and that it was of no importance. Of one's ideals, strug-
> gles, deprivations, sorrows and joys, it could only be said that they
> were chemic compulsions, something which for some inexplicable
> reason responded to and resulted from the hope of pleasure and
> the fear of pain. . . . With a gloomy eye I began to watch how
> the chemical—and their children, the mechanical—forces operated
> through man and outside him, and this under my very eye.

Also before his eyes "were always those regions of indescribable poverty
and indescribable wealth" which led him to write: "Never in my life, neither before nor since, in New York, Chicago, or elsewhere, was the vast gap
which divides the rich from the poor in America brought so vividly home to
me. . . . True, all men had not the brains to seize upon and make use of that
which was put before them, but again, not all men of brains had the blessing
of opportunity as had these few men." Then came this self-analysis, only
part of which was to prove prophetic: "How to get up in the world and be
somebody was my own thought now, and yet I knew that wealth was not for
me. The best I should ever do was to think and dream, standing aloof as a
spectator." A spectator Dreiser was throughout his life, but he was also an
observer; and as soon as he began to record his observations, he became a
novelist. As for wealth—although he would never be another Carnegie,
Frick, or Rockefeller, thirty years later, following the publication of his
sixth novel, he had what was to him a fortune: about $25,000 in royalties
for the first six months' sale of the book and $90,000 for the motion picture
rights. *An American Tragedy,* though never on the best-seller list, was far
more popular than any of his other novels had been on publication.

More significantly, reviewers and critics who had not been favorably
disposed toward Dreiser's earlier books found something praiseworthy in
this one. After a quarter-century during which he had stood his ground in
spite of disheartening attacks from almost all sides, he was "somebody"—he
had got "up in the world." And what he had risen from, what he had seen
and felt and thought on his way up—the themes, the types of people, the
events that make up his novels—we find touched on in the following passages from the first two pages of *An American Tragedy.*

Dusk—of a summer night. And the tall walls of the commercial heart of an American city of perhaps 400,000 inhabitants—such walls as in time may linger as a fable. And up the broad street, now comparatively hushed, a little band of six,—a man of about fifty, short, stout, with bushy hair protruding from under a round black felt hat, a most unimportant-looking little person, who carried a small portable organ such as is customarily used by street preachers and singers. And with him a woman perhaps five years his junior, taller, not so broad, but solid of frame and vigorous, very plain in face and dress, and yet not homely, leading with one hand a small boy of seven and in the other carrying a Bible and several hymn books. With these three, but walking independently behind, was a girl of fifteen, a boy of twelve and another girl of nine, all following obediently, but not too enthusiastically, in the wake of the others. . . . As they sang, [the] nondescript and indifferent street audience gazed, held by the peculiarity of such an unimportant-looking family publicly raising its collective voice against the vast skepticism and apathy of life.

The "little band of six" provide an interesting example of Dreiser's way of fusing elements from his own background and elements drawn from observation. The father, modeled in part on a street preacher seen years before in Kansas City, where *An American Tragedy* opens, also calls to mind his own overreligious father, whose appearance "bespoke more of failure than anything else." Mrs. Griffiths reminds the reader of Dreiser's mother; and her boy Clyde is what Dreiser describes himself as having been: a "mother child." The elder Dreisers had appeared previously in *Jennie Gerhardt*, as had other members of the family, including one of Theodore's sisters, whom we see again here as Hester Griffiths. Both the Dreiser and the Griffiths families were "always hard-up, never very well clothed, and deprived of many comforts and pleasures which seemed common enough to others." It was partly this sense of deprivation that developed in Clyde Griffiths the same longing that Dreiser had experienced: ". . . the gay pairs of young people, laughing and jesting, and the 'kids' staring, all troubled him with a sense of something different, better, more beautiful than his . . . life."

One of Dreiser's own early characteristics is represented in this opening chapter of *An American Tragedy*, not by Clyde's reaction, but by that of members of the street audience. "Some were interested or moved sympathetically by the rather tame and inadequate figure of the girl at the organ, others by the impractical and materially inefficient texture of the father. . . ." From childhood, Dreiser had longed for better things for himself; but at the same time that he envied and admired the wealthy and the strong, he sympathized with the poor and the weak. In one of his autobiographical volumes he recalls his childish pity for his mother when he noticed her worn and broken shoes. "That," he said, "was the birth of sympathy and tenderness in me." In St. Louis just prior to his departure for Pittsburgh, he was looking at everything about him with a covetous eye, depressed by the thought that he would never know prosperity and fame. He was also "filled with an intense sympathy for the woes of others, life in all its helpless degradation and poverty, the unsatisfied dreams of people . . . the things they were compelled to endure. . . ."

A further passage from the first page of *An American Tragedy* will lead us into a consideration of Dreiser's most significant novels: "And the tall walls of the commercial heart of an American city. . . ." From boyhood, Dreiser had been fascinated by cities—first Chicago, then St. Louis, later Pittsburgh, and still later New York. In the opening chapter of *Sister Carrie* he recalls the thrill of his first visit to Chicago, and the setting of that novel is urban throughout. The action in *Jennie Gerhardt* takes place in Columbus, Cleveland, and Chicago. The first two volumes of the "trilogy of desire"— *The Financier* and *The Titan*—have Philadelphia and Chicago as their settings. And it is Kansas City and Chicago that start Clyde on his way in *An American Tragedy*. In the first two and the last of these five novels Dreiser makes plain the isolation of the individual surrounded by the "tall walls." But it is against the "commercial heart" not only of the city but of America that he is inveighing in all his major novels.

Dreiser was not the first American novelist to focus his attention on post-Civil War urbanization and its attendant corruptions. Henry Blake Fuller had dealt with Chicago in *The Cliff-Dwellers* and *With the Procession*, and Frank Norris had presented detailed pictures of parts of San Francisco in *McTeague* and *The Octopus* and of Chicago in *The Pit*. More important than these writers, however, because of his influence on youthful readers, was the man who promised the inevitable rise to fame and fortune of any boy, provided that he arrived in the city equipped with pure heart and a full set of copybook maxims, worked hard, remained honest, and saved the life of a millionaire's daughter. Jed the Poorhouse Boy, Paul the Peddler, Julius the Street Boy, Phil the Fiddler, Tom the Bootblack, Ragged Dick— all these Horatio Alger heroes helped to promote the tradition that arose out of the success of Fisk, Gould, Carnegie, Vanderbilt, and Rockefeller. Between 1866 and the end of the nineteenth century, about 130 Alger titles attained an aggregate sale of between sixteen and seventeen million copies. And the majority of these books, though warning against the pitfalls of urban life, held out the hope of success to American boyhood.

As a boy in Evansville, Indiana, Dreiser had read Alger's *Brave and Bold, Luck and Pluck, Work and Win,* as well as Hill's *Manual of Etiquette and Social and Commercial Forms,* in which he found "pictures of cities and great buildings and of men who began as nothing in this great sad world but rose by honesty and industry and thrift and kind thoughts and deeds to be great." As an adolescent in Chicago, he was burning to use the brain that an older man of considerable knowledge assured him he had, so that he "might share in the material splendors which everywhere, as I saw, men were struggling for." Some time later, while employed as a bill collector for a household furnishings company, he realized that he could not satisfy his dreams on $14.00 a week. "I had to take them out in longing or derive some way of raising the money." Desiring especially an overcoat with satin lining, the better to fit in his dream world, he withheld surplus payments collected from customers, intending to repay gradually the amount thus "borrowed." But he was soon discovered and discharged. Such an experience, though it stopped far short of murder, must have given him some insight into the Clyde Griffiths who would come into being about thirty-five years later.

By this time Dreiser was "nearly hypochondriacal on the subjects of poverty, loneliness, the want of the creature comforts and pleasures of life. The mere thought of having enough to eat and to wear and to do had something of paradise about it." Experience had marked him with a horror of being without work; but he soon obtained the first of a succession of reportorial assignments on Chicago newspapers. From Chicago he was to proceed by way of St. Louis to Pittsburgh, where he first tried his hand at creative writing, and where, as he later told Burton Rascoe, he decided to become a novelist and to use as a subject one of the industrial or business geniuses of the period.

For about five years after his Pittsburgh experiences, Dreiser was an editor and a free-lance writer of magazine articles in New York. Before finding an opportunity of any kind, he lived precariously and fearfully on the edge of poverty. As he sat one wintry day on a park bench, he sensed anew the overwhelming contrast between the world of the unemployed and destitute whom he saw around him and the world of success symbolized by the tall buildings near at hand. While writing *Sister Carrie* in 1899 he was to remember this experience.

What happened to Dreiser's first novel is a commentary on American culture. *Sister Carrie* had been accepted for publication by Frank Norris, the reader for Doubleday, and Dreiser had signed a contract with the publisher. But the story goes that Doubleday handed a copy to his wife; she read it; and the trouble began. Mrs. Doubleday found the novel so shocking that her husband, prompted by her reaction, issued only enough copies to abide by the contract, and advertised the book not at all. What impressed Mrs. Doubleday and some other early readers as immoral was the fact that Carrie Meeber, an innocent young woman from a farm, was permitted to rise to fame unpunished in spite of having lived, without benefit of clergy, for a short time with Drouet, then for three years with Hurstwood. Dreiser's

first contribution to the development of the American novel was his refusal
to pretend that a girl who had Carrie's experiences inevitably paid for
her misdemeanors while the man went on his merry way. Only eight years
before the first printing of *Sister Carrie,* Stephen Crane's *Maggie,* the brief
story of a girl driven to prostitution, had shocked the few who read it; but
the fact that Maggie ended her life by drowning should have satisfied those
whose moral views demanded that the wages of sin must be death. Carrie
Meeber was not made to suffer because Dreiser based her story on the experience of his own sister, deceived by a man who, like Hurstwood, had
stolen from his employers and taken her with him to New York. Dreiser
knew that his sister's irregular behavior did not end in degradation or death.

There are few more gripping chapters in fiction than those tracing the
decline of Hurstwood. When Carrie meets him, he is the successful, well-
to-do, respected manager of a Chicago restaurant. But once the couple are
in New York, Carrie's fortunes rise and Hurstwood's steadily sink: loss of
work, dwindling funds, apathy, loneliness, beggary, and then his last appearance in the small, close room that he has rented for fifteen cents,
obtained by begging. "After a few moments, in which he reviewed nothing,
but merely hesitated, he turned the gas on again, but applied no match.
Even then he stood there, hidden wholly in the kindness that is night,
while the uprising fumes filled the room. When the odour reached his nos-
trils, he quit his attitude and fumbled for the bed. 'What's the use?' he
said weakly, as he stretched himself to rest." Our minds go back to the
man who, as he rubbed elbows with the destitute in a New York City park,
shuddered with a fear of what might be ahead for him. It was at that
moment, Dreiser said, "that Hurstwood was born." And in the words of
F. O. Matthiessen, it was "with Hurstwood" that "Dreiser began his chief
contribution to American literature."

For seven years after its first publication, *Sister Carrie* was almost completely unknown to American readers. Dreiser's frustration over the fate
of his first novel (from which he had netted less than $100) led to a
severe breakdown; he was unable to work, except sporadically, for three
years. Eventually he obtained editorial employment, and for six years,
while producing potboilers for periodicals, he was connected with various
magazines that published the unrealistic kind of fiction which he could
not bring himself to write. Nothing seems more incongruous than the
Naturalistic author of *Sister Carrie,* complete with pince-nez and "nobby"
clothes, serving as the editor of *The Delineator,* a magazine for properly
domesticated women. His secretary said he looked "Not as I had expected
an editor to look. More like a College professor." In spite of that handicap,
Dreiser was a most successful editor; the wonder is that throughout this
period the spirit and feeling that had caused him to write *Sister Carrie*

survived. When his connection with the Butterick publications was severed, he settled down to work on *Jennie Gerhardt*.

In the early part of this novel, Dreiser drew heavily upon the predicament of his family during his childhood. The experience of Jennie, an unwed mother, is based upon that of one of his sisters, but in her sweetness of character she is modeled upon his mother. Whereas in *Sister Carrie*, Hurstwood seems to be the chief character, here Jennie is really the heroine. For many years the mistress of a rich man, she cannot become his wife because of their difference in station. Although Dreiser does not gloss over the illicitness of their relationship, he refrains from creating scenes of passion. In both *Sister Carrie* and *Jennie Gerhardt* he is reticent about physical love. He no more intended to pander to the taste of those who desired a vicarious and salacious thrill than he intended to represent the attraction of men and women for each other as leading to a sexless relationship. He was presenting the truth as he saw it and knew it.

If in his next two novels—*The Financier* and *The Titan*—Dreiser places greater emphasis on sex (though here too his scenes of physical passion seem quite restrained today), he does so because his "hero," Frank Cowperwood, must behave as did his original, Charles Yerkes. Dreiser chose Yerkes from among the financial buccaneers of nineteenth-century America because he needed a central character different from most of the robber barons, who have been characterized as discreet and well controlled, their strongest lust their appetite for money. Yerkes was very much a man of flesh and blood, as the entry in the *Dictionary of American Biography* will show. This biographical account of the man who gained control of the transit systems in Philadelphia and Chicago proves how closely Dreiser followed the facts. Yet Cowperwood is not merely an academic representation of Yerkes; to a degree, in his sexual drive, he is Dreiser himself. Speaking of his brother Paul, Dreiser once remarked: "I have never known a man more interested in women from the sex point of view (unless perchance it might be myself). . . ." Perhaps for this reason he is able to be objective and never condemnatory in treating Cowperwood's affairs. But more important than this slight resemblance is the significance of Cowperwood as a symbol at once of the kind of success that the young Dreiser had dreamed about and of the injustice practiced on the weak by the strong and clever.

Whereas the history of Hurstwood had been an Alger story in reverse, *The Financier* gets under way in typical Alger fashion. Frank Cowperwood is not poor; but it is largely on his own initiative that he scores his first successes; and because of the promise he shows, he wins the approval and help of his superiors. In the first chapter, however, he adopts a philosophy that can hardly be considered Horatian, basing his conclusion on a drama that he has witnessed. On his way to and from school he passed a fish market, at the front of which stood a tank containing a squid and a lobster. Day by day, little by little, the lobster preyed upon the squid, until finally the squid was no more. Young Frank began to analyze the incident. " 'How is life organized? ' he asked himself. ' Things lived on each other—that was it. Lobsters lived on squids and other things. What lived on lobsters? Men, of course! . . . And what lived on men? . . . Was it other men? . . . Sure, men lived on men.' " And with this decision, the boy's feet are set on the path not of Paul the Peddler but of the ruthless financiers of the Gilded Age. He is on the way to becoming a Naturalistic strong man; like Jack London's physical brutes, he will illustrate the meaning of the Darwinian-Spencerian phrase "the survival of the fittest."

Since both *The Financier* and *The Titan* are biographical, the plot line was laid down for Dreiser in advance. By reading all the newspaper reports of the life of Yerkes, he obtained the major incidents. As for the character of the man, it is said that for all his crimes against American cities, there was something fresh and ingratiating about Yerkes, possibly because he was not hypocritical. "The secret of success in my business," he frankly stated, "is to buy old junk, fix it up a little, and unload it upon the other fellows." When attacked for not making available more seats in trolleys, he remarked, "It is the strap-hanger who pays the dividend." Cowperwood is not so plainspoken, nor does he win the reader's sympathy. But Dreiser tries to make him understandable. Cowperwood's motto is, "I satisfy myself." In applying this motto to his sexual behavior, he explains his motivation in terms of the "chemic compulsions" or "chemisms" that Dreiser mentioned so frequently after reading Spencer. And this behavior among businessmen and politicians is what we should expect of a man who sees life in terms of the relations between squids and lobsters.

If *The Financier* and *The Titan* are read in succession, the second seems hardly more than a duplication of the first. Stuart P. Sherman's characterization of *The Titan* might apply equally well to its predecessor: a "huge club-sandwich composed of slices of business alternating with erotic episodes." Both contain a wealth of detail which make them good social history. The American businessman had been pictured in various guises by a number of novelists including William Dean Howells and Frank Norris. But Cowperwood dwarfs all others as a ruthless financial pirate, a character stranger than fiction because founded on fact. Once we have acknowledged the historical significance of these two novels, we must admit they are not lively reading. Dreiser manages to create a certain amount of suspense in *The Financier*, and there are melodramatic scenes in *The Titan*; but the average reader will find both less fascinating than *Sister Carrie* and *Jennie Gerhardt*, perhaps because of lack of sympathy for Cowperwood.

During the remaining twenty-one years of his life Dreiser was to com-

plete only three more novels. One, *The Bulwark*, was published posthu-
mously. (*The Stoic*, volume three of the "trilogy of desire," was also published after his death, though unfinished.) The two which appeared during
his lifetime are *The "Genius"* and *An American Tragedy*. The first of these
is considered by many to be the weakest of his novels, perhaps because it is
too autobiographical. The fact that the New York Society for the Suppres-
sion of Vice banned *The "Genius"* temporarily in 1916 is of interest chiefly
because it emphasizes Dreiser's unique contribution to American literature.
From 1900 he had been fighting what amounted to a one-man battle against
the prudishness of American literary taste. He steadfastly refused to omit
or change a situation or a detail which he had experienced or observed
and therefore knew to be true. He would not falsify to please the Mrs.
Doubledays or the John S. Sumners. Some later writer would have fought
such a battle if Dreiser had not done so; but no one before him had dared
or had lived to press the fight. The Hemingways, Dos Passoses, Faulkners,
Farrells have Dreiser to thank for having won for them the right to present
life honestly.

Soon after the publication of *The "Genius"* Stuart P. Sherman, a fairly
conservative critic, wrote of the Dreiser novels that had thus far appeared:
"These five works constitute a singularly homogeneous mass of fiction. I
do not find any moral value in them, nor any memorable beauty . . . but
I am greatly impressed by them as serious representatives of a new note
in American literature. . . ." This "new note" Sherman discusses at some
length, concluding: "It would make for clearness in our discussions of
contemporary fiction if we withheld the title of 'realist' from a writer like
Mr. Dreiser, and called him, as Zola called himself, a 'naturalist' . . . . A
naturalistic novel is based upon a theory of animal behavior. Since a theory
of animal behavior can never be an adequate basis for a representation of the
life of man in contemporary society, such a representation is an artistic
blunder. . . . And so one turns with relief from Mr. Dreiser's novels to the
morning papers."

Ten year later Sherman opened his review of *An American Tragedy* as
follows:

> Youngsters who think to shelve Dreiser with the retiring title of
> 'the grand old man of realism' reckon without his large, stolid,
> literary ambition, which to my mind, is his most salient and ad-
> mirable moral characteristic. As a novelist he has been silent these
> ten years. And now with his familiar huge plantigrade tread he
> comes lumbering down the trail with a massive 800-page American
> tragedy which makes the performances of most of his rivals and
> successors look like capering accomplishments of rabbits and squir-
> rels. . . . I do not know where else in American fiction one can find

the situation here presented dealt with so fearlessly, so intelligently, so exhaustively, so veraciously, and therefore, with such unexceptionable moral effect.

Undoubtedly Sherman had grown in tolerance and understanding during the World War I period. And following the war, as a book reviewer he could hardly wave aside the novels that were coming from the pens of Sinclair Lewis, Dos Passos, and numerous writers, more popular in their day than now, all of whom revealed at least traces of the Naturalism of which Sherman had formerly disapproved. At the same time, it must be admitted that *An American Tragedy* is different from Dreiser's previous novels in one important respect. Ironically enough, what raised it so high in Sherman's estimation was the fact that it is, in its objectivity, the most Naturalistic novel that Dreiser ever wrote. In each of the preceding novels, editorializing or philosophizing comments are numerous. The improvement in Dreiser's technique Sherman noted; but he attributed it to a change from "barbaric naturalism" to "tragic realism." Actually, objectivity had always been the first desideratum of the American Naturalists, though probably none before this had so completely attained it.

When Sherman after reading *The "Genius"* turned "with relief . . . to the morning papers," he was going to the source—the objective source—from which Dreiser drew much of his material not only for the Cowperwood novels but for his greatest work, *An American Tragedy*. Not that he was waiting for a sensational news story that would furnish a plot. His problem was to choose from among at least sixteen murder cases which had been reported at length during the preceding thirty years the one that would best suit his theme. Ever since becoming a newspaperman, he had noticed how frequently a certain type of crime was committed: the murder of a socially and financially inferior girl by a lover who hoped, by removing her, to be free to marry a wealthy girl of higher social station. In each instance, as Dreiser saw it, the guilty man was himself a victim—a victim of the American Dream. The only kind of success recognized in America was that measured by money and social position. Perhaps because he found the material easily accessible, Dreiser decided to concentrate on the case of Chester Gillette, who had been electrocuted on March 20, 1908, for the drowning of a girl named Grace Brown in Big Moose Lake.

The story of *An American Tragedy* can be briefly summarized. Clyde Griffiths, the son of street-corner evangelists, has already begun at the age of twelve to think of how he may better himself. After a short period in his early teens as a helper in a drugstore, he obtains a job as a bellboy in a leading Kansas City hotel. He finds his first taste of worldly life most exciting. But this experience ends suddenly following an automobile accident in which a child is killed; although Clyde was not the driver of the borrowed car, he fears punishment and disgrace, and flees. In Chicago, while working as bellboy in the Union League Club, he meets the wealthy uncle of whom he has often heard his parents speak, and whom he impresses so favorably that he is eventually offered employment in the uncle's collar and shirt factory in New York state. At this point, Horatio Alger seems to be winning. But Clyde finds that his wealthy relatives are not disposed to pay much attention to him. Once they have entertained him at dinner, they consider their social obligation ended. He does not enjoy his work, he has no friends, and he finds his days dull and depressing, even after he is promoted to a foremanship. He yearns for companionship, especially feminine; but without the help of his relatives he has no way of meeting other young women than those in the factory, and company rules forbid showing an interest in them.

One week end, seeking entertainment at a near-by park, he comes upon Roberta Alden, the only girl by whom he has been attracted at the factory. Ironically, in view of what is to follow, they spend a happy, innocent hour rowing on the lake. After this, Clyde and Roberta continue to meet after working hours; but the coming of cold weather, when parks are closed and long walks in the country are out of the question, raises a problem. Eventually, now much in love with Clyde, Roberta allows him to visit her in her rooms and becomes his mistress. Shortly after, Sondra Finchley, one of the Griffiths set, invites Clyde to a social function, chiefly to annoy his cousin Gilbert, who dislikes Clyde. This incident leads to a succession of invitations from other members of the socially elite, and it encourages Clyde to think of a possible future with Sondra, who represents beauty, wealth, and social prestige. About the time it becomes apparent that Sondra is in love with him, Roberta tells him that she is pregnant and demands that he provide for her. From the beginning, Clyde has been determined not to let his relationship with Roberta lead to marriage; now that his prospects with Sondra and her world are so bright, he persuades Roberta to try certain drugs and then to appeal to a doctor to perform an illegal operation. These attempts are unsuccessful. When it is obvious that Roberta will expose him to his relatives unless he marries her, he is stirred by a newspaper story to plan an "accidental" drowning. Rowing to an isolated spot on an Adirondack lake, he finds himself at the crucial moment afraid to carry out his plan; but as Roberta gets to her feet and moves toward him, he raises his hand, and, not actually intending to do so, throws her off balance. The boat capsizes; and as Roberta sinks beneath the surface, Clyde swims to shore. Within a few hours he is apprehended. Following a lengthy trial, in which the political ambition of the district attorney plays a more important part than a desire to see justice done, Clyde is convicted of murder and goes to the electric chair.

Although Dreiser read the published accounts of the Chester Gillette case, especially the report of the trial, he made some changes and additions. The opening section of *An American Tragedy* was undoubtedly suggested by the early life of Dreiser himself. Clyde as a bellboy is modeled upon a bellboy whom Dreiser had encountered in Chicago. Various details connected with the drowning scene are changed. And the period is the twenties instead of the first decade of the century. What is most important is that whereas Gillette actually committed murder, Clyde accidentally strikes the blow that sends Roberta to her death. Thus, as has been said, "the evidence is of a crime against Christian morals rather than against written law." This change makes it possible for Dreiser to label Clyde a mental and moral coward rather than a killer. Whether Clyde's weakness entitles him to pity is a matter which the individual reader must decide. Certainly, though we are told that Sondra and most of her crowd found Clyde "charming," we see little evidence of his charm; we have been with him since childhood days and know him to have no definite character, but only a vague desire to rise in the world in accordance with American standards. To quote Carl Van Doren, "Nobody tells him what to be. Everybody tells him what to have."

If we compare Clyde with the central characters in the other novels, we observe that though he is the least qualified to succeed, he is motivated by the same incentive as Carrie Meeber and Frank Cowperwood. Carrie, a poor girl from the country, was looking for something better than she had known. She stepped outside the recognized moral code to get her start, and after Hurstwood's fortunes began to decline, she would undoubtedly have gone the way of Crane's Maggie to prostitution and death if she had not possessed some talent as an actress. Frank Cowperwood, as a boy from a family that was reasonably well off, had a better chance than Carrie at the outset; and having a sharp intelligence, no conscience, and the determination to satisfy himself, he was bound to succeed. Clyde, with no gift or talent, and certainly no strength of character, could only trust to luck. Without attempting to influence the reader to judge Clyde, Dreiser follows him with underlying pity from his beginnings as a seemingly good-hearted boy to his end as a seeming murderer. His luck had been against him. And even though his own weakness was ultimately responsible for his downfall, yet with a different start in life, better educational opportunities, a few more dollars each week in his pay envelope, but most of all, a different criterion of success, what might his life have been? That the dividing line is thin is suggested by the fact that Dreiser received many letters from people who wrote: "Clyde Griffiths might have been me."

But also deserving of pity is Roberta Alden, whom most critics seem to ignore. Her background was no better than Clyde's—or, for that matter, than Carrie Meeber's or Jennie Gerhardt's—and she had the same dreams.

The irony of her situation is that as she sees her association with Clyde as a step up the social ladder, he himself is frustrated because he cannot attain the status of his uncle's family and their circle. The awful aloneness of Roberta after she senses that Clyde no longer really loves her Dreiser handles with tenderness and understanding. It is more of an American tragedy— tragedy for America, perhaps a tragedy for which America was responsible —that Roberta, an attractive, sweet-natured, kind-hearted girl, who had once shown the potentiality of realizing her dreams, should go to her lonely death because of the mores and rules of her society, than that Clyde should be driven to plan her death because of his desire to improve himself. She is both a more winning and a more living character than Clyde.

The same cannot be said of the other girl. When Dreiser attempted to deal with a social group outside his own orbit, he was not successful. Sondra Finchley and her gay circle speak and behave like characters in a travesty on life among the Four Hundred. Perhaps Dreiser's lack of sympathy with such people made it impossible for him to bring them to life, but the fact that he had never mingled in that society is probably an adequate explanation. His other leading characters and the numerous minor middle-class figures are realistically conceived. In the creation of those in subordinate roles, Dreiser uses countless details to good effect. Typical is the introduction of the country coroner, who "was lethargically turning the leaves of a mail-order catalogue for which his wife had asked him to write. And while deciphering from its pages the price of shoes, jackets, hats, and caps for his five omnivorous children, a greatcoat for himself of soothing proportions, high collar, broad belt, large, impressive buttons chancing to take his eye, he had paused to consider regretfully that the family budget of $3,000 a year would never permit of so great a luxury this coming winter, particularly since his wife, Ella, had had her mind upon a fur coat for at least three winters past." In a novel of lesser proportions this material might seem superfluous, but by the time we are two-thirds through *An American Tragedy*, we are not surprised to find such a passage. A reader of Dreiser recognizes the accumulation of details as part of his method of making the reader believe that something *is*.

How necessary and effective a part of Dreiser's method it is can be appreciated from a reading of his posthumous novel *The Bulwark*, which at times gives the impression of being a skeleton of a novel, lacking the flesh that Dreiser's documentation had always before provided. But if in this respect the method is somewhat changed, the same cannot be said so unreservedly of the style. The ineptitudes for which Dreiser had been criticized ever since he began to write novels are evident in *The Bulwark*. The deficiencies of his style are so obvious as to call for no special comment: the passages that I have quoted contain illustrations of those faults. But in his best novels Dreiser rises above his style; and if the first principle of success in literature is sincerity, then in spite of his style he must be judged a success. As Sherwood Anderson said, "If you look for word-love in his book you'll get left. Love of human beings you'll find. It's a finer attribute in the end."

Near the close of *The Bulwark*, Solon Barnes, the central character, while walking in his garden, observes the behavior of a green fly, and ponders.

> Why was this beautiful creature, whose design so delighted him, compelled to feed upon another living creature, a beautiful flower? . . . And now so fascinated was he by his meditations on this problem that he not only gazed and examined the plant and the fly, but proceeded to look about for other wonders. . . . Then, after bending down and examining a blade of grass here, a climbing vine there, a minute flower, lovely and yet as inexplicable as his green fly, he turned in a kind of religious awe and wonder. Surely there must be a Creative Divinity, and so a purpose behind all of this variety and beauty and tragedy of life.

Whether Solon Barnes, approaching the end of his days, is here expressing a conclusion that Dreiser himself had reached is a matter for conjecture. Whatever may have been his personal thought, the view of life presented at the conclusion of *The Bulwark* is vastly different from that at the beginning of *The Financier*. In replacing the squid and the lobster with the flower and the fly, Dreiser closes his career as a Naturalistic writer.

VALUES AND DIFFICULTIES
IN THE ART OF MARCEL PROUST

JAMES T. STEEN

I SUPPOSE EVERYONE COMES AT ONE TIME or another to reflect upon that great human blessing of not knowing the future in advance. I wonder, for instance, how Tolstoy would have felt had he known that there would one day be developed for the United States Army a machine claimed to be capable of reading *War and Peace* in five minutes. I myself can't help wondering what that machine will do after it has read *War and Peace*. Perhaps it will go to see the motion picture and annoy some less sophisticated machine at its elbow by announcing that the book was much better. And I can't help thinking also about Marcel Proust, a melancholy individual at best; though he might have been heartened to know that his *Remembrance of Things Past* would give that machine pause for a full twenty minutes, would he have been gratified at the sacrifice of the last twelve years of his life for *that*? James Joyce, on the other hand, might have felt positively smug. For though he might have suffered the vision of his *Ulysses* coming quickly to bay before the automaton, he would have known in his heart that *Finnegan's Wake* would shatter the machine.

It does seem an affliction of many of the most significant modern works of the imagination that they are more famous for their difficulties than for their pleasures, that they are far more talked about than read. Some difficulty has probably always accompanied greatness in works of art, but it seems never to have continued to impinge upon their glories so much as it has recently. We have in T. S. Eliot, for instance, an example of a modern poet who has to be explained not only to the average reader—if there is such a thing as an average reader of T. S. Eliot—but also to the well-educated one. Whether or not difficulty has become actually one of the criteria of greatness in art at this point in our culture would be a study in itself. But there is this to be observed: that in the novel particularly, since the impact of the industrial and scientific revolutions upon human life and thought, many of our most important writers seem to have become intent upon driving their works to the limit of understanding in one direction or another. Thus, observes Malcolm Cowley (*The New Republic*, July 9, 1956),

> . . . we have the limit of scientific naturalism in Zola (though later writers have outdone him in mere brutality), and the limit of invaded privacy . . . in Molly Bloom's inner dialogue (at the end of *Ulysses*). Joyce himself would go deeper into the psyche, by merging thoughts into dreams, but in *Finnegan's Wake* he would also reach the limit of difficulty, for any book intended to be read and understood. The limit of controlled fantasy was probably reached in Kafka; at least one suspects that anything more fantastic than *The Castle* would not be a novel. The limit of conscious vision was reached in Henry James, and something like the limit . . . of writing directed by the subconscious in William Faulkner; the limit of intricate formal structure in Thomas Mann; the limit of historical scope in *War and Peace*; that of geographical scope in *U.S.A.* And the limit of minute analysis was reached . . . in *The Remembrance of Things Past*, and quite possibly the limit of sheer bulk for any novel conceived as an architectural unit.

Now I'm not prepared to stand behind all of that, but I believe it is true that in *The Remembrance of Things Past* Proust developed height of structure and depth of analysis to the extent that they decidedly restrict the book's readership and thus deprive it of a full general impact. Unless a reader be as obsessed with towering structure and microscopic analysis as Proust was, he may not be willing to go the limit of these seven volumes, with their interminable sentences and paragraphs endlessly radiating from some single point of interest while the narrative stands still. And as for other *writers*, only the most foolhardy and careless of public acceptance would dream of imitating Proust on the grand scale. Rather they may take as their watchword the comment of Joseph Conrad, "I don't think there has ever been in the whole of literature such an example of the power of analysis, and I feel safe in saying that there will never be another." This is sheer admiration for sheer genius, and it expresses the kind of awe which one is bound to feel when he reads Proust; but what it amounts to is a recognition that Proust has done this sort of thing once and for all.

It is, of course, just these qualities of vast scope and complexity that make *The Remembrance of Things Past* the unique and splendid reading experience that it is. But it is equally true that they yield up their rewards only upon a complete reading of the work. For instance, although the opening pages are clearly enough titled "Overture," we cannot know until we turn the final page just how exactly they are a microcosm of the whole work, and that in the narrator's idling reveries we are being introduced to all the characters, themes, and settings which are to come. The narrator, the writer, in recalling the difficulties he had once had as a child in trying to go to sleep without his mother's goodnight kiss, because she was entertaining dinner guests downstairs, remembers that someone had had the happy idea of giving him, for the evenings when he was abnormally wretched,

> . . . a magic lantern, which used to be set on top of my lamp. In the manner of the master-builders of Gothic days it substituted for the opaqueness of my walls an impalpable iridescence, supernatural phenomena of many colors, in which legends were depicted, as on a shifting and transitory window. But my sorrows were only increased, because this change of lighting destroyed . . . the customary impression I had formed of my room, thanks to which the room itself, but for the torture of having to go to bed in it, had become quite endurable. For now I no longer recognized it, and I became uneasy, as though I were in a room in some hotel or furnished lodging, in a place where I had just arrived, by train, for the first time.

We cannot know at this point that in the final volume the narrator, now middle-aged, will have again reached this same painful psychic state, when, at the last of the brilliant parties of the great world of Paris, he suddenly finds himself surrounded by total strangers, who are really all familiar people terribly transformed by the magic lantern of time, time which he cannot believe has passed so swiftly, and which he sadly discovers has ravaged him in the same way.

When in the first volume we learn of the jealous tortures which Charles Swann inflicts upon himself and the cocotte Odette, tortures which are doubly agonizing to the refined Swann because he knows that Odette is not his "style" of woman, we cannot know that at a point much later in the work the narrator himself will undergo identical tortures because of a girl identically unworthy of him.

We cannot feel the full emotional brunt of the novel or know the psychological truths which it unlocks until we have followed its entire course and can stand back and look at its patterning of emotional recurrences. For this book does not depend upon the traditional kind of continuity in fiction. It does not consist simply of a motion-picture-like succession of incidents, starting at one point in time and progressing toward another. It is rather like a succession of brilliantly colored slides, each projected upon our minds for as long as the operator cares to hold it in the projector, then replaced by another, in no apparent logical or sequential order, but only according to some indecipherable plan of the operator.

Time, for Proust, as for the philosopher Bergson, was not simply a standard of measurement with which men could by agreement mark off the days of their lives. It was a mysterious creative force, with duration and mobility of its own, a force whose intervention between events not only separated them from one another, but gave them their very meaning and thus told one the character of his life. What it had done became apparent only when the individual, in some unwitting repetition of a sense-experience, suddenly found himself transported back into a moment of the past, so that he was occupying for an instant both past and present simultaneously, with a great flood of released memories telling him the truth of his life. "It was this conception of time as incarnate," says Proust through his narrator in the final volume, "of past years as still close held within us, which I was now determined to bring out into such bold relief in my book."

Thus we have the famous and vital episodes of the tasting of the tea and cookie, the stepping on the uneven flagstones, the touching of the damask napkin to the lips, the clinking of the spoon against the cup, and several others. The spontaneous excursions into the past which these sense-experiences set off, Proust called "involuntary memory," and it was this subtle mental action and the intuitive vision which it inspired that motivated his novel, rather than the more familiar intentional remembering and historical recounting. And this is one reason why we may find it a totally new reading experience, and one whose difficulties may at first outweigh its charms.

I have found it helpful, in understanding the nature of *The Remembrance of Things Past*, to compare its creation, not with that of other works of fiction, but with the building of the great Gothic cathedrals of Normandy and Ile de France, which Proust loved and studied so thoroughly. Just as those inspired builders attempted through material means to express man's inarticulate cravings, so Proust attempted through language to express the inexpressible. And as they accomplished the impossible through the persistent efforts of generations of men, so Proust drove himself to his accomplishment through twelve fanatical years of writing and rewriting. Just as they so often changed their grand schemes midway, according to the inspirations of new generations, so Proust changed his novel radically in the making. He had originally planned three volumes. The first, *Swann's Way*, was to tell of the comfortable middle-class world in which the narrator Marcel, like Proust himself, lived his childhood. Its hero, Charles Swann, was Marcel's boyhood model of the educated, civilized, and thoroughly charming individual that he himself hoped to become. The second, *The Guermantes Way*, would tell of the fascinating world of high Parisian society, into whose mysteries Marcel hoped to penetrate by virtue of the charm he would attain by studying Charles Swann. The stars of this aristocratic world would be the Duchess and Duke of Guermantes, the quintessence of physical beauty and worldly elegance. And the third volume, *The Past Recaptured*, would reconcile the two worlds through intermarriage, while it would satisfy Marcel's longing to be a part of both worlds by virtue of his having united them in a work of art, the book itself.

Swann's Way was printed and the second volume was in type when the outbreak of war in 1914 stopped publication. Thereupon Proust, like a second generation of men taking up the work on a half-finished cathedral and turning it to their purposes, began a vast revision and expansion of his original scheme under the impetus of France's agony in the war and of the deepened introversion which it had brought about in him. When printing was resumed, he had expanded the original sixteen hundred pages to over four thousand, had more than doubled the number of volumes, and had radically changed the character of the work in its final parts in accordance with the darkened mood of Europe during the war.

And again, as most of the Gothic cathedrals were left unfinished, often purposely, in symbolism of the imperfectibility of human achievements, so *The Remembrance of Things Past* was left unfinished, though not purposely, at Proust's death in 1922. The grand scheme was complete and the final volume written, but the rewriting, which to Proust was always a matter of urgency, had progressed only midway into the fourth volume.

Proust once admitted that he had actually planned to give to the different sections of the novel the names of the parts of a cathedral—The Porch, The Windows in the Apse, and so forth—but that he found these pretentious. Certainly though, in its bulk, its stillness, and its recurrent motifs the book does suggest a cathedral. In its deep glooms, too, and its sudden bursts of light and color. And in the presence in it of so many of the other arts—music, painting, sculpture, pageantry, stained glass. The characters themselves seem to be attached to its great linguistic walls and towers and corbels like so many saints and gargoyles. They come alive for us because of Proust's strenuous, imaginative efforts to discover the emotional life which lies behind their masks, just as the statuary of those medieval cathedrals, static and unmoving as it is, can come alive for the viewer only through a long and careful imaginative perusal. And though it is true that Proust sings no mass, so to speak, in his novel—he was deeply moral but never conventionally religious—his moral sense is nevertheless everywhere implicit in the style and structure of his work, as surely as the moral quality of the cathedral builders speaks out of the stones and glass in which they worked, even when their religion is no longer practiced in the spaces they enclosed.

It is this huge, motionless, and quietly illuminated quality of *The Re-*

membrance of Things Past, then, which sets it magnificently apart in fiction, making it inaccessible to the run of modern readers, and surely restricting it as a literary influence. No creative writer would dream of imitating it, even if he were willing to give twelve years, and eventually his life itself, to the effort; no one today would attempt Proust's intricate analysis or his long, sinuous sentences, which demand constant attention of a reader, and present to the practicing writer the discouraging spectacle of a technique carried to its limit.

Yet all of this is not to say that *The Remembrance of Things Past* is a difficult book in the way that *Ulysses* and *The Castle*, for instance, are difficult. Proust was an extremely articulate writer in the traditional sense, not a linguistic innovator. He was rather a refiner of language, probably to the absolute limit of refinement. One may more easily see how really lucid a writer he was in his critical essays on Ruskin, Flaubert, and Baudelaire. But even in *The Remembrance of Things Past*, where the aesthetic purpose is dominant, his ideas are given a beautiful clarity all their own, so that it has been possible to extract an entire volume *(The Maxims of Marcel Proust)* of statements of general truths from the pages of the novel.

And in fact it was by its fine synthesis of the intellectual and the aesthetic that this work made its initial impact upon the writers of the twenties. If the more difficult Joyce was to become the avant-garde reading of that day, Proust was directly in the center of intellectual fashion. Forbidding as he must have been to the general reader, he was just what the intellectuals were looking for. What Freud, Einstein, and Bergson had demonstrated scientifically and logically, Proust demonstrated aesthetically. His book embodied the ideas which animated the twentieth century. Major trends in politics, science, art, psychology, morals, philosophy, warfare—the whole trend of society and the human mind was there. The very mood of the new "lost generation" was there. If we can think of the intellectual world of the twenties as a gigantic vacuum caused by the explosion of World War I, we may visualize all of the new ideas, discoveries, and attitudes which till then had been held in check by die-hard tradition, and by the rude necessities of the war, suddenly rushing in. Liberation and chaos arrived simultaneously. It was a time of high excitement and deep uncertainty. Proust's coolly reasoned melancholy and his immense grasp of idea ordered the chaos and gave the intellectuals their book.

In the last three years of his life, those years immediately following the war, he became world-famous even though only half his work was yet published. In England, Arnold Bennett and John Galsworthy saw him as the lineal follower of Dickens and George Eliot, two of Proust's own early idols. Middleton Murry spoke of the great ascetic and educational value of the book. In Germany, Curtius wrote, "A new era in the history of great novel-writing has opened with Proust . . . he imposes himself on our intelligence no less than on our imagination." Enthusiastic Americans, Thornton Wilder among the most vocal, at once turned Proust into a classic. At home in France, among his rivals as well as his friends, he was stubbornly resisted as well as championed. But unquestionably, as André Maurois has put it, "The massive figure of Proust came more and more, in foreign eyes, to dominate the first half of the twentieth century, as the massive figure of Balzac dominated the nineteenth."

In addition to setting an intellectual example for his contemporaries, and striking their prevailing mood, Proust also helped to establish a fashion for the new generation of novelists in point of view, the capital "I." If society was now forced to relax its grip upon the individual, the writer, as a result, could no longer look to society alone as the center of his concerns. The self had become the nerve-center of the novel. And Proust, who had discovered the special value of this viewpoint even before the war, became, through his obsessively introspective narrator, the natural teacher. In this respect, and in respect to his ideas and mood, we can easily say, with Edmund Wilson, that Proust "subsumes" much European, British, and American fiction of the 1920's and thirties, and that as a kind of compendium of modern concepts in his prodigious style, he became himself a modern concept, for which we now have in literary jargon the word "Proustian."

Beyond this, to look for specific examples of Proust's influence becomes a pointless search. For the period between the wars now shows itself to us more and more as a truncated literary period. With rare exceptions like Kafka and possibly Faulkner, it did not produce new writers of fiction of the order of Proust, Mann, Joyce, and Lawrence. Though it presented a busy and variegated literary scene, it was also marked by mediocrity, fragility, self-consciousness, and thwarted literary careers. As far as Proust was concerned, it was able to adopt his viewpoint, to toy with the ideas which he mastered, and above all to assume his pessimism. But in no one do we find anything like his wonderful talent for language, his ability to convey massively his personal sense of the beauty and humor and pathos of life. The limited and somewhat perverted use to which the writers of that period were able or willing to put their reading of Proust seems to be epitomized in the critical response of Edmund Wilson to the book in 1931: "*The Remembrance of Things Past*, in spite of all its humor and beauty, is one of the gloomiest books ever written." Seen by the reader or the writer in this way, its structural and stylistic genius subordinated to its prevailing mood, the book could never exert the profound influence of which it is capable, an influence which never has been realized, and which now may never be.

Now I know that I have slipped into contradictions which I cannot resolve. I've said that the influence of *The Remembrance of Things Past* has been seriously limited by its difficulty, and then that it is not a difficult book and has been a decided influence, and then that its influence has been slight, in view of what it might have been. I don't mean to defend these contradictions, but I must tell you that I am far from the first who has fallen by the wayside in talking or writing about Proust and his novel. Out of a general agreement that Proust was indeed a Frenchman who lived from 1871 to 1922, and that he did indeed write a novel which we know in English as *The Remembrance of Things Past*, have come several thousand conflicting opinions about the meaning of the novel, the value of it, the influence of it, the sources of it, and so on.

Even about Proust himself we seem to be sure of nothing, although his life appears to be thoroughly documented. We are told that he was thin, frail, and ghost-like but also that he was rather sturdily built, full-faced, and of rugged constitution. That he was rather tall, and that he was quite short. That he was misanthropic, and that he was extremely kind, considerate, and loving. That he was fastidious, and that he was dirty. That he was obsessed with the fear of dying, that he longed to die, and that he was quite indifferent to death. That his book is ugly and grossly overwritten, and that it is of rare beauty and almost perfect proportions.

In short, speaking or writing of Proust is rather like invading Russia—it can be done, but it isn't likely that it can be gotten away with. Sooner or later the critic of Proust is swallowed up in the vastness of a huge and richly variegated work written by one of the most complex creatures ever to occupy a high position in a field already crowded with eccentrics. The conflicting views of Proust and his book are all apparently true and supportable. But they cannot be singled out without upsetting the larger truth that Proust's book, like the man himself, is in some essential way contradictory.

It is true of Proust himself, for instance, that as a young man he was markedly dreamy, sensitive, and introspective. But it appears to be equally true that he was normally aggressive. He was drawn not only to his own mind and memory and to the art of the past, to books, paintings, music, and cathedrals, and to the genealogy of the ancient houses of France, but also to the world of the present, a world in which he took at one time large part. Like the fashionable people of Paris whom he so admired, he had his own wide but select circle of friends—many of them noted people—and some enemies. He strove ambitiously for literary recognition. (An amusing anecdote is told by Somerset Maugham, in one of his prefaces, about Proust's having written a review of his own work for a journal which had been slow in responding to the publication of *The Remembrance of Things Past*. He submitted it under the name of another well-known writer, who was in turn told by the editor of the journal, "I must refuse your article. Marcel is a valued friend. He would never forgive me if I printed a criticism of his master-work that was so perfunctory and unsympathetic.") He joined and for a time led one of the literary factions of Paris, and did journalistic battle with other factions. He once even fought a duel with another writer over a remark he had made about that writer's work. (Both missed their shots.)

However, what is particularly significant about the young Proust is that he had a fondness for his own mother which we can only call inordinate, and that he depended upon her, far more than the outside world realized, for his morale in that world. After her untimely death his life took its decisive turn. He began to retire from the world and set about organizing some of his desultory writings into the form of an autobiographical novel. He was, as we have seen, well along with this when his country became engaged in war, a new kind of war, which quickly assumed ghastly proportions. Proust had been since childhood seriously afflicted with asthma, and though he did attempt military service, he was found to be physically unfit. But the brutality of the war, and the knowledge that his friends and compatriots were killing and being killed in a mass slaughter which was beyond the military power of either side to resolve, revolted him so that he became completely introverted, retiring almost totally from the world and entering into a way of life which must be seen as morbid and self-destructive.

In this dark psychic state he undertook the vast expansion of his novel which I have already referred to. We cannot know whether that original novel would have been more than a melancholy and rather idyllic collection of memories, but now it became a portrayal of human nature and society so subtle, so shocking, so darkened with misanthropy, and at the same time so entertaining, that many readers refuse to accept it as true, while others are convinced that it was meant only as a continuation of the high comedy of the early volumes. Some find it positively distasteful to read beyond the end of the third volume *(The Guermantes Way)*, the point at which the dark turn seems to have been taken.

To fulfil the obsession which his novel had now become, Proust shut himself away, first in the famous cork-lined room in the family apartments, and later in a shabby rented room, with only a devoted family servant to look after him. He worked by night and seldom went out. When he did, it was usually in the small hours of the morning. He adopted the bizarre habits of sleeping fully clothed, even to shoes and gloves, and wearing the heaviest clothing when he went out, even in warm weather. He subsisted almost entirely on coffee, some foolish friend having assured him that the mind is clearest when the stomach is empty. He began to use narcotics to induce sleep during the day. The ravages of this kind of life can be clearly seen in a first-hand report given by Havelock Ellis, in *From Rousseau to Proust*, of Proust's arrival at a party, in 1922, just ten months before his death:

Proust . . . arrived at two in the morning, during a pause in the
concert being given by one of the new pianists of the Stravinsky
school. The doors opened, and an apparition appeared which was
Proust . . . . [He] gave the impression of an exhumed corpse in remarkable preservation, in all black clothes, of the cut of 1890, hang-
ing much too large on his emaciated figure. His dead black hair was
worn much too long; the great dark rings round his eyes and his
waxlike long hands . . . the fingers as straight as if they were not
articulated, and his whispering voice—all made an impression which
actually for a time threw a chill over the gathering. [The host]
conversed with him for a half-hour or more, and in all that time
Proust evidently talked genealogy . . . he knows all the family trees
in France, who married who, and so on; to compliment the musician
of the evening he asked him if he would be good enough to go on
playing until eight or nine in the morning. He made this mild request towards four A.M., when most of the guests were very sleepy
. . . and saying goodbye; but of course it was midday to Proust, who
was beginning to be wide awake. When he gives people appointments the hour is always round four A.M.

At those strange appointments he would call in friends, acquaintances,
and servants, consult with them about details of the material for his novel,
and send them out on new researches. A servant sent to the home of an old
friend of Proust, at any hour of the day or night, might be instructed to
deliver the following speech: "Monsieur has sent me to ask Monsieur and
Madame what became of Shelley's heart." He consulted women endlessly
on the subject of fashions which had long since been outmoded, and apparently he used them mercilessly. "But my dear Marcel," a victim was once
heard to plead, "it's been twenty years since I wore that hat! I've no longer
got it." "That, Madame," answered Proust, "I find it hard to believe. No,
the truth is, you don't want to show it to me. It's there, but you've made
up your mind to provoke me. That makes me very unhappy." The visitors
could sometimes scarcely see their "host" through the clouds of fumigations
which were kept going constantly because of the asthma. The bed on which
Proust sat propped up with pillows was in great disorder, covered with
hundreds of pages of manuscript, as were the floor and the furniture throughout the room.

Now it is of course unfair to portray a once elegant and vivacious person
only as he appeared in the last stages of exhaustion, malnutrition, and
narcotic poisoning. Proust was that strange nocturnal creature only during
a small part of his life, and even then, those who truly knew him and knew
what he was about must have recognized beneath the ravaged exterior the
man who, as Lewis Galantiere has phrased it in his introduction to *Swann's
Way*, ". . . moved by a passion for his art, had the organizing genius of a

Napoleon . . . a serenity of soul which raised him far above himself . . . and that unshakable will without which the consummation of vast creative projects is impossible." I cite the 1922 picture of Proust as self-destroyed only by way of explaining the presence of so many contradictions in what we read and hear about him, an explanation which is further borne out when we read the novel itself and realize that it bears no correspondence whatsoever to the emaciation of its dying author, and further, that its gloominess bears to its great beauty only the incidental correspondence that the interior gloom of a cathedral bears to its total grandeur.

The essential "contradiction" of Proust and his book which I have spoken of is just that he has revealed his peculiar apprehension of life to us so comprehensively, so minutely, and so *essentially*, in comparison with the more tailored, message-driven, and symbol-studded kinds of *representative* fiction to which we probably will have become accustomed before we come to Proust, that we simply may not be able, or willing, to "take him in" at first. "It is important," says E. M. Forster, "when tackling Proust to be patient and intelligent. He makes no concessions to stupidity. He expects a constant awareness both from the mind and from the senses. . . .[But] he has raised that rather tiresome word 'art' to an importance and a sublimity that we cannot neglect."

It is as a sublimely original work of art, then, rather than specifically as fiction, autobiography, social history, or philosophical argument, that we must view and study this great book if we want to see and learn from its greatness. Proust's ideas have surely made their way into many minds, and his mood has affected many hearts. But ideas change and moods fade; and stories are finally told once too often. What remains when these have lost their power to please or to teach is the stamp of the artist himself—call it his moral quality, or his talent—upon the materials in which he has worked.

Proust's artistry is far too huge a subject to be treated in any fulness here, but I want at least to mention a few of its notable features so as to make clear the degree to which some well-known aesthetic methods characterize Proust's writing.

I have already spoken of the architectural quality of the work—Proust called the writing of the book his *"travaux d'architecte"*—and that, I suppose, is the ruling artistic conception embodied in it. A smaller but most characteristic one is his use of "aesthetic distance." I don't mean simply the author's interposing of a narrator between himself and his reader. I mean specifically his frequent interposing of some veiling material or atmospheric condition between the narrator and what he sees. For instance, the young Marcel of the book first sees the little girl with whom he is to fall in love, Gilberte Swann, through the tall hedge which surrounds her father's estate. He first sees Mme. de Guermantes, with whom also he is to fall in love, through the deep interior of a church, alternately lightened and darkened by the passing of clouds over the sun on a windy day. And notice here how the atmospheric condition is correlated with the emotional essence of the moment (and also how three of the other arts—music, painting, and poetry—are drawn into the passage) :

> . . . the sun, bursting out again from behind a threatening cloud and darting the full force of its rays . . . into the sacristy, shed a geranium glow over the red carpet . . . along which Mme. de Guermantes advanced, and covered its woollen texture with a nap of rosy velvet, a bloom of light, giving it that sort of tenderness, of solemn sweetness in the pomp of a joyful celebration, which characterize certain pages of *Lohengrin*, certain paintings by Carpaccio, and make us understand how Baudelaire was able to apply to the sound of the trumpet the epithet "delicious."

Similarly, the young Marcel sees the lovely Mme. Swann, with whom also he is to fall in love, walking on the Avenue du Bois on a May afternoon, "in the depths of the liquid transparency and of the luminous glaze of the shadow which her [mauve] parasol cast over her." He witnesses the strange scene between Mlle. Vinteuil and her friend from within the bushes outside her open window at twilight, just hidden from the yellow glow of her lamp. When he describes the sea from his window at Rivebelle, he is particularly conscious of the quality which the glass and the framing of the window add to his sense of the view. And turning around, he continues to describe the outside scene as it is reflected in the glass doors of bookcases along the inner wall of his room. There are literally hundreds of such instances in the book, instances in which the material through which or by means of which the scene makes its way to the viewer's eye is shown to embody or transmit the emotional content of the scene. And these visual instances correspond to Proust's concept of time itself, in which time becomes understood as a material invisibly interposed between oneself and the essence of one's life.

Another characteristic of Proust's artistry is his considerable use of the techniques of Impressionism, among them his way of applying primary "colors" in a myriad minute "daubs" to create total effects, and particularly his love of presenting multiple views of the same scene, under varying conditions of light and shade and season, so as to catch its essence the more truthfully, moment by moment, rather than in one arbitrary or ideal view. To adequately illustrate this second technique would require quotations of impracticable length, but a glimpse of it may be seen in a part of that description of the sea which I mentioned above (and here again we may also observe Proust's habit of reinforcing his descriptions by referring to the other arts) :

I went into my room. Regularly as the season advanced, the picture that I found there in my window had changed. At first it was broad daylight, and dark only if the weather was bad. And then, in the greenish glass which it distended with the curve of its round waves, the sea, set among the iron uprights of my window like a piece of stained glass in its leads, ravelled out over all the deep rocky border of the bay little plumed triangles of an unmoving spray delineated with the delicacy of a feather or a downy breast from Pisanello's pencil, and fixed in that white, unalterable, creamy enamel which is used to depict fallen snow in Galle's glass.

Presently the days grew shorter and at the moment when I entered my room the violet sky seemed branded with the stiff, geometrical, travelling, effulgent figure of the sun . . . leaning over the sea from the hinge of the horizon as a sacred picture leans over a high altar, while the different parts of the western sky exposed in the fronts of the low mahogany bookcases that ran along the walls . . . seemed like those different scenes which some old master executed long ago . . . whose separate panes are now exhibited side by side upon the wall of a museum gallery. . . .

A few weeks later, when I went upstairs, the sun had already set. . . . Over the sea, quite near the shore, were trying to rise, one beyond another . . . vapors of a pitchy blackness but also of the polish and consistency of agate . . . I was on all sides surrounded by pictures of the sea.

Although this is only a very small part of the total passage, it shows, I think, a striking resemblance between Proust's artistic method and the Impressionism, say, of Debussy, in his multiple picturing of the sea in *La Mer*, and certainly that of Monet in his "series" paintings, particularly those of the water lilies at Giverny and the cathedral of Rouen. In these works the attempt has been, like that of Proust in his novel, distinctly not to "recognize" but to *see*, not just in spatial dimension but also in time.

And then I just want to mention briefly a third facet of Proust's artistry, his particular sensitivity to the values of figurative language. Here again, the selection of one instance from among the thousands in the book may seem futile, but I think that the following passage may serve some purpose. The boy Marcel and his beloved grandmother have visited a park, where she has become suddenly ill. They have gone immediately to a doctor and Marcel has been told, out of his grandmother's hearing, that she has had a stroke and that there is not the slightest hope for her. They have started homeward. And here the simile seems remarkably well chosen, in both scope and particulars, to convey powerfully and sharply the dominant emotion of the moment, in this case a refined and overwhelming sorrow: "The sun was sinking. It burnished an interminable wall along which our cab had to pass before reaching the street in which we lived, a wall against which the shadow cast by the setting sun of horse and carriage stood out in black on a ruddy background, like a funeral car on some Pompeian terra-cotta."

I know that these few brief illustrations can only dimly suggest the artistry of Proust's writing, but add to these several consciously artistic techniques which pervade the actual style of the book the abundance of material in it about the arts and culture in general, and the number of characters directly associated with the field of art—the painter Elstir, the novelist Bergotte, the actresses Berma and Rachel, the composer Vinteuil, the violinist Morel, the connoisseur Charlus, the narrator-writer Marcel, and others—and one begins to get some notion of the degree to which the reading of this work is an aesthetic as well as an intellectual experience.

Proust was an extremely cultivated person as well as a rarely talented one. His prodigious powers of observation, intellect, and recall, his genuine love of the act of writing, and his endless capacity for rewriting were fed by a broad and deep humanistic education and were brought to bear upon an irresistible natural curiosity about all matters aesthetic. The range of his reading was immense, and his acquaintance among writers and artists was wide. He studied the art of the past and present assiduously, and his intuitive understanding of the ways of art was said to be uncanny. I am sorry that I haven't time to provide the details of these sweeping views, but the picture they give of Proust as a thoroughly cultivated genius is, I believe, what Van Wyck Brooks meant when he spoke of the "supremacy of talent" which made Proust one of "the rulers of the literary mind of his generation."

In all of this he seems to me to stand as something of a contradiction in the twentieth century—an individual of genius, great accomplishment, *and* great cultivation, a great nonspecialist, representing in the art of fiction the culmination and the end of a cultural age, just as those parts of his novel which deal with social manners and mores represent the culmination and the end of the old European society. This is what makes his book so huge and singular a reading experience and one that is inaccessible to many moderns. He is not the writer for those who prefer more facile or straitened ways. His writing is not "streamlined," and it cannot be labeled so that we will know in advance what we are getting. Terms such as Realism, Romanticism, Naturalism, Symbolism, and the like, fall away before the immensity of what he has done, an accomplishment which, like that of other books that are both difficult and wonderful, we may see relegated more and more to service as a standard of measurement of the reading capacity, not of people, but of machines like the one I mentioned at the beginning of this talk.

To be sure, there are many things that one might wish Proust had never bothered to put into his book, for he can try one's patience and the endurance of one's intelligence. But impracticable as he must be seen to be as a model for writers in an age of specialization, he is an invaluable and practically unique teacher for readers, and I, for one, am inclined to agree, at least in my more capable hours, with Somerset Maugham's declaration that he "can read every word with interest" and in any event "would sooner be bored by Proust than amused by any other writer."

Proust himself would probably have been amused at anyone's efforts to "place" him, high or low, in literary ranks. "There is nothing fixed or certain," he wrote in his final volume, "by which the reasoning intelligence may judge works of art; one can easily demonstrate anything he wishes." No, he would have managed to tell us far more clearly and less patronizingly than I have of the value of himself and his book for readers in any time. In fact he has told us, in a passage toward the end of the book that is characteristic of his wisdom and his art: "I had a more modest opinion of my book and it would be incorrect to say even that I was thinking of those who might read it as 'my readers.' For . . . they would not be my readers but readers of themselves, my book serving merely as a sort of magnifying glass . . . so that I would give them the means of reading in their own selves. Consequently, I would not ask them to praise or disparise me but only to tell me if it is as I say, if the words they read in themselves are, indeed, the same as I have written."

What one sees in *The Remembrance of Things Past*, then, if he sees anything, is himself, hugely magnified, transformed sometimes beautifully, sometimes grotesquely. What view, seen for the first time, could be more difficult or more fascinating?